A Students' Guide to Japanese Grammar

【英文】間違えやすい日本語語法

Naomi Hanaoka McGloin
マクグロイン花岡直美

Taishukan Publishing Company

A STUDENTS' GUIDE TO
JAPANESE GRAMMAR

© Copyright 1989
Naomi Hanaoka McGloin

PREFACE

Errors made by students are a valuable tool in foreign language teaching as they are extremely revealing of the differences between the target language and the native language and of the inner workings of the target language. This book will zero in on selected problem areas in Japanese grammar as seen in the errors frequently made by English-speaking students of Japanese and offer in-depth explications of these points.

Items selected here are all taken from mistakes made by my intermediate and advanced students. Needless to say, they continue to make mistakes in mechanical aspects of grammar such as not using proper conjugation in certain constructions. However, most of their mistakes at this point are attributable to their inability to differentiate the usages of two or more similar grammatical forms which do not have obvious corresponding distinctions in English. The primary aim of this book, then, is to explicate usage differences between similar constructions involving particles, temporal expressions, sentence-final expressions, conjunctions and others.

This book is intended primarily for students of Japanese who have a basic knowledge of Japanese but would like to get a better grasp of Japanese grammar. It should prove useful also for the teachers of Japanese.

In studying and teaching Japanese grammar, I have benefited greatly from the wealth of recent findings in Japanese Linguistics. Many of these findings are incorporated in this book and pertinent literature is acknowledged at the end of relevant entries. I would, in particular, like to acknowledge Kuno's *The Structure of the Japanese Language* and Alfonso's *Japanese Language Patterns*, which have provided me with many insights into Japanese grammar.

Finally I would like to express my appreciation to Chisato Kitagawa and Hiroko Terakura for reading an earlier version and giving me valuable comments; to Prof. Kazuko Inoue for her encouragement and help; to Mr. Jun'ichi Yoneyama of Taishukan publishing Co. for his editorial help; and to my husband, Jim, for proofreading. Most of all, I am grateful to all the students I taught both at the University of Michigan and at the University of Wisconsin-Madison for asking many invaluable questions.

Madison, Wisconsin
July, 1988

TABLE OF CONTENTS

教師のために
(FOR TEACHERS)

　日本語を外国語として教える教師にとって，学生の犯す誤用は非常に貴重な教材である。誤用はもちろん学生の不勉強によるものも多いが，教師側の説明不足，または日本語と外国語との本質的な違いによるものも多い。こちらが与えた規則に従って学生が作った文が不自然な場合，どうして不自然なのか説明に困る場合も多いが，そういう問題について考えていくうちに教師自身の日本語に対する理解も深まっていくのである。

　誤用にはいろいろなレベルのものがあり，語彙の誤用など特に大きな問題もあるが，ここでは英語を母国語とする学生の間違いを通して，間違えやすい語法，問題となりやすい語法のいくつかに焦点をあててみた。基本的な文法を一応マスターしていると思われる中級・上級の学生でも，その語法の間違いの多くは，基本的なレベルの類義表現の区別がよくできていないことに根ざしているようである。類義表現を中心に，特に学生にとって問題となりやすいものを選んで，学生に分かりやすいように例文の説明を中心にまとめてみた。学生の誤用が目立つのは，特に助詞，時の表現，接続の表現などである。以下，それらを中心にいくつか主な点を概説してみたいと思う。

時の表現・仮定表現

　　　誤用が多いのは，やはり時を表わす「た」と「る(う)」の使い分けであろう。特にこれらが関係節，擬似関係節に表われた場合，注意を要する。英語の過去形は常に過去のことを表わすが，日本語の「た」は過去と共に完了を表わす。つまり，[...V_1 -た/る ...V_2] という構造の場合，「た」を使うと V_1 が V_2 以前に

行われたという意味になる場合が多いのである。次のような対比を与えて説明すべきであろう。

(1) a．日本へ行った人と話した。
　　b．日本へ行く人と話した。
(2) a．私は，あした母の作ったお弁当を食べる。
　　b．私は，あした母の作るお弁当を食べる。

例文(1)では，「行った」を使うと「日本へ行って帰ってきた人と話した」という意味であるが，「行く」を使うと「日本へこれから行く人と話した」という意味になる。また，(2)では「作った」という過去形が可能であるが，その場合発話の段階ではお弁当はまだ作られていない訳だから，「作った」は「食べる」という動作の前に完了しているということを示す。(2)のような場合，「作る」も可能であるが，「作った」のほうがより自然な文であろう。例文(1b)，(2a)のような時制の使い方は英語にないので，特に注意をする必要がある。

　同じようなことは，「時」で導かれた節にも言える。

(3) a．バスを降りる時，注意した。
　　b．バスを降りた時，注意した。

「降りる」を使うと，「バスを降りつつ」または「バスを降りる直前」という意味であるが，「降りた」を使うと，「バスを降りたあと注意した」という意味である。

　さて，英語では，2つの文を時間的関係として捉える場合（when S_1, S_2）と，仮定条件として捉える場合（if S_1, S_2）とでは明瞭な区別がある。"When you go to Japan, you should visit Kyoto." と言えば，話し手は聞き手が日本へ行くことを前提として言っているが，"If you go to Japan, you should visit Kyoto."というと，話し手は聞き手が日本へ行くかどうか知らないが，もし行くことがあれば，という気持ちで言っている。日本語では，このどちらの場合も「日本へ行ったら，京都へ行ってごらんなさい」で，「たら」で表わせる。

　日本語の条件文には，「たら」「と」「ば」「なら」の4つがあ

る。このうち「たら」と「と」は時間的関係を示すことも仮定条件を示すこともできる。聞き手が日本へ行くことを知っていて（前提として）発話すれば，時間的関係を示すことになるし，そういう前提がない場合は，仮定条件となる。

　この中で，最も使用範囲の広いのは「たら」なので，大抵の場合は「たら」を使っておけば間違いはないが，それぞれの違いはおおまかに言うと次のようになる。

　「と」は前件と後件が習慣的・論理的な関係にあることを示す。「春になると，あたたかくなる」，「夜コーヒーを飲むと，眠れなくなる」のように，前件が起こると必ず当然のこととして後件が起こるという気持ちである。「たら」では，「た」が完了を示すことでも分かるように，前件のあとで後件が起こるという時間的前後関係が問題になっている。「なら」は誰か他の人が言ったことを受けて，それが本当に事実なら次のことが起こるだろうという意味。「ば」は後件を実現するための必要条件を示す。学生には次のような例を出して，それぞれがどのような状況で使われるのか説明する必要がある。

(4)　a．あなたが読んだら，
　　　b．あなたが読むんなら，
　　　　　　　　　　　　　　　　私も読みます。
　　　c．あなたが読めば，
　　　d．*あなたが読むと，

　　［*印は，その文が非文法的であること，⁷印は，文法性・適格性について疑いがあることを示す。］

(4a)は，「あなたが読む」という行為が実現されたら，そのあとで「私も読む」という意味である。(4b)は，聞き手が「読む」と言った状況で，話し手が「あなたが言ったことが正しいなら，私も読む」と言っている。(4b)の場合には「私が読む」ことは聞き手の「読む」と言った断言にかかっているだけなので，時間的に「私が読む」のが「あなたが読む」ことの前に起こってもいい。(4c)は「私が読む」ための条件は「あなたが読む」ということだから，「あなたが読まなければ，私は読まない」とい

う意を含んでいる。「と」は後件に話し手の意志を表わす表現が
くると，（4d）のように不適格な文となる。

　先にも述べたように，「と」には時間的関係を示す用法がある
ので，「時」との区別で問題になることが多い。例えば次のよう
な誤用文を参照されたい。

　(5) ＊説明すると，たくさん例をあげます。
　(6) ＊日本では人の家へ遊びに行くと，おみやげを持ってい
　　　きます。
　(7)[?]＊日本の地下鉄に乗る時，動けないぐらいこんでいる。
　(8)[?]＊その時のことを思い出す時に，いい気持ちになった。

まず，「と」を使うと後件が前件の<u>あと</u>に起こらなければならな
い。したがって，前件と後件が<u>同時</u>に起こる場合，または後件
が前件の前に起こる場合には「時」が適格である。例文(5)と(6)
が不適格なのはこの理由による。

　また，[S₁時，S₂] では，<u>いつ</u> S₂ が起こったかという点に焦点が
あるが，[S₁と，S₂] では，S₁ と S₂ の間に何らかの関連性が認めら
れる。それは，S₁ が起こると必ず S₂ が起こるというような関連
性でもあり，また「S₁ が起こったら何が起こったか —— S₂ が起こ
った」というような関連性でもある。例文(8)では，<u>いつ</u>いい気持
ちになったかが問題なのではなく，その時のことを思い出すと
必然的にいい気持ちになったのだから，「と」が適格である。

　動詞に「いる」がつくと，動作の進行，動作完了後の状態の
継続，経験，習慣的状態など動詞によって，種々の意味用法が
あるが，英語を母国語とする学生にとって一番問題になるのは，
「ている」形が動作完了後の状態継続を表わす場合だろう。動詞
が移動を表わす動詞（行く，来るなど），着衣動詞（着る，かぶ
るなど），瞬間動詞（結婚する，死ぬ，持つ，忘れるなど）の場
合，その「ている」形は，ある動作が完了したあとの状態を表
わす。例えば，「田中さんは結婚している」と言うと，「田中さ
んは結婚して，今，結婚しているという状態にある」ので，「結
婚式をしている最中」という意味ではない。「スミスさんは，今
日本へ行っている」というと，「日本にいる」のであって，「日

本へ行く途中」という意味ではない。「*私は兄が一人います
が，兄は結婚しません」のような基本的な使い方から，「*本当
に愛したら，そんなことは言わなかったでしょう」のような使
い方まで誤用が多い。

　これと関連して注意すべきものに，「考える」とか「思う」と
いう動詞の「る」形，「ている」形がある。何か意見を述べる場
合，次の例のように，主語が一人称の場合は「る」形，主語が
三人称の場合は「ている」形を伴うのが普通である。

(9)　a．私は，それは間違いだと思う。
　　　b．田中さんは，それは間違いだと思っている。

この規則を適用して，学生はよく主語が三人称の場合，過去に
なっても「ていた」を使うが，不自然になることが多いので注
意を要する。

(10)　A：太郎は，どうして，その時，嘘をついたんでしょ
　　　　　うか。
　　　B：本当のことを言うと，誰も相手にしてくれないと
$\left\{ \begin{array}{l} 思った \\ 思っていた \end{array} \right\}$からでしょう。

(10)では「思った」のほうが自然である。確かに「思っていた」
も使えるが，その場合は太郎が前からずっとそう思っていたと
いう意味になる。

接続の表現

　文と文を正しく結ぶというのは非常に難しい作業で，間違い
が多い。学生の間違いで目立つのは「のに」の誤用である。「の
に」は，非常に主観的な表現で，話者が期待したことと事実が
違う場合，話者の驚き，不満，失望などの感情を表わす。次の
例を参照されたい。

(1)　勉強したのに，できなかった。

(2)　日本人なのに，漢字が書けない。

(1)では，勉強したんだからもっとできてもよかったのに，という話者の失望，不満の気持ちが出ている。(2)でも，日本人だから漢字が書けるはずなのに書けないとはおかしいという非難の気持ちが表わされている。したがって，例文(3)，(4)のように客観的な叙述では「のに」は不適当である。

(3)　このアパートは $\left\{ \begin{array}{l} \text{*きれいなのに,} \\ \text{きれいだけれど,} \end{array} \right\}$ 便利じゃない。

(4)　家のうらてに庭がありました。庭は大きくなかった
$\left\{ \begin{array}{l} \text{*のに,} \\ \text{けれど,} \end{array} \right\}$ 池と小さな木がたくさんありました。

　また，学生は自分がしたことを話す時によく「のに」を使うが，「のに」を使うと自分の行為に対して，非難，失望の気持ちを表わすことになるので不自然になることが多い。これは特に注意をしたい。

　学生の誤用には，日本語を母国語とする者には考えもつかないような間違いも多いが，それは，日本語を外国語の翻訳で考えているのが1つの大きな原因であろう。例えば，次の誤用例を参照していただきたい。

(5)　*ビールを飲まなくても，バーへ行った。

(6)　私の家族は，フォンタナという町に住んでいます。*その町は，大きくなくても，とてもきれいな町です。

普通，「けれど」を使うべきところである。このような誤用が出てくるのは，学生が「〜ても」も「けれど」も"even though"という英語で覚えているからだろう。ちなみに，「〜ても」は過去の事実を述べる場合，"even though"と訳されるが，「前件にどんな状況があっても後件が起こる」という意味を含んでいるので，(5)，(6)のような客観的な事実の描写には不適当である。学生の誤用例を見て改めて考えさせられた語法の一例である。

　ある行為が主体の意志で実現可能とみなされるかどうかは，しばしば語法記述の中で重要な役割を占める。例えば，目的の「～ために」と「～ように」がその一例である。「Xのために」のXは，話者の意志で実現できる行為，「Xのように」のXは，話者の意志で実現できないとみなされる行為である。したがって，状態動詞，可能動詞，無意志動詞などは，典型的に「ように」と共起する。学生はしばしば「*日本語が上手になるために日本へ行った」というような文を作るが，日本語が上手になるかどうかは意志では実現できないことなので，「ように」が妥当である。

助詞

　助詞で問題になるのは，やはり「が」と「は」の使い分けである。「が」と「は」については多くのすぐれた論文もあり，教科書などでもかなり詳しく説明してあるので，それらを参照していただきたいが，久野 (1973) では，「主題」と「対照」の「は」，「総記」と「中立叙述」と「目的格」の「が」を認めている。文の主題は，誰/何のことを話しているのか聞き手にも話し手にも分かると判断できる名詞句でなければならない。先行文脈にでてきたもの，発話の状況から推測できるもの（これ，それ，など），人々の一般知識としてあるものなどは「主題」になれるが，初出名詞でも，談話の話題，または，先行文脈にでてきたものから推測できるもの（例えば，家族の話をしている時の「母」「父」など）も，「主題」になれることも忘れてはならない。

　次のような例文を参考にしていただきたい。

　(1)　a．太郎は学生だ。
　　　　b．太郎が学生だ。

(1a) では「太郎は何か」と，「何か」の部分に焦点をあてているのに対し，(1b) では「誰が学生なのか」と「誰が」の部分に焦

点がある。

(2)　a．駅はそこにあります。
　　　b．あそこに駅があります。

(2a)は「駅はどこにあるか」という質問の答えとして使える。
(2b)は「駅があるかどうか」が問題になっているので、「駅」は
主題になりえない。この場合の「が」は中立叙述の「が」であ
ろう。

(3)　きのう男の人が来ました。その男の人は黒い帽子をか
　　　ぶっていました。

　最初の「男の人」は、聞き手にとってはこの時初めて聞いた
のであって、主題にはなりえない。したがって「が」で導入す
ることになる。しかし、一度導入されると、そのあとからは主
題になりえるので「は」が使える。

(4)　誰が(*は)来ましたか。

学生は「誰、何」などの疑問詞の場合も「は」を誤用するが、
「誰」は主題にはなりえないから「は」はおかしい。

(5)　コーヒーを飲みましたか。
　　　いいえ、コーヒーは(^{??}を)飲みませんでした。

学生は否定文に「は」を入れないことが多いが、普通、否定文
には「は」を使うのが自然である。否定文では、「は」を使うこ
とによって「コーヒーは飲まなかったが、他のものは飲んだ」
という意味を表わすことが多い。

(6)　$\left\{\begin{array}{l}\text{子供が}\\\text{子供は}\end{array}\right\}$病気だから学校へ行けません。

学生の誤用に非常に多いのが、従属節の中の「は」の使用であ
る。従属節の主語が「が」になることは特に強調すべきである。
(6)の例のように、「は」になると従属節の外へ出てしまうからで

ある。

その他，助詞は日本語の中でも誤用の多いところだが，かなり上級になっても「で」と「に」の間違いが目立つ。「に」は存在の場所を示し，「で」は動作の行われる場所を示すといえばことは簡単にすみそうだが，「*東京で住んでいます」「*ホテルで泊まりました」のような間違いを頻繁に耳にする。同じ動詞でも「に」と「で」で意味が違ってくるので注意して教えるべきである。

 (7) a．家にあります。(物が家に存在するという意味)
    b．家であります。(パーティーなどの催し物が家で行われるという意味)
 (8) a．駅の前で待っています。
    b．駅の前に立っています。
 (9) a．ここで書いてください。(ここは場所を指す)
    b．ここに書いてください。(ここは書類など書く紙を指す)

「に」を使った場合は，動作が係っていても，究極的には人や事物がそこにいる/あるという意識につながる。

文末表現

 文末表現で一番問題になるのは「～のです」という表現であろう。「のです」の基本的機能は「話者がある情報を既知情報と想定して提示する」というようなところにあるのではないかと思われるが，「のです」の持つ意味合いは文脈によって，かなり変わってくるので，教える際は種々の文脈での意味合いの違いを提示するのが良いと思う。

 一般的に「のです」は「説明」を与える，と言える。例えば，「頭が痛いんです」と言えば，話し手が元気がないのは頭が痛いのが理由だと説明していると言える。しかし，「説明」と言えない「のです」も数多い。「パーティーへ行くんですか」という質

間の場合，よそ行きの洋服を着ている人に対して言った場合は「説明」と言えるが，何も状況がない場合(例えば，人からその人がパーティーへ行くらしいと聞いた時)にも言える。その場合には，話者の推定・想定を表わしている。

　また，「のです」は話し手が自分の経験などを述べる時によく使われるが，そのような場合には別に説明すべき状況もない。そのような「のです」は，会話の相手との協調を計る機能があり，相手にやさしく働きかけるものである。学生は，とかくこの機能を敷衍して，「のです」をつけると，何でもやさしく丁寧に聞こえると思うのか，この種の誤用が多いので注意したいものである。例えば，電話をかけた時，「*もしもし，先生はいらっしゃるんでしょうか」とか「夏休みはどうでしたか」に対して，「*ええ，とても良かったんです」などと答えるのがその例である。

　さらに，「のです」を使うと，やさしく聞こえるどころか非難しているようで失礼になることもあるので，これも注意すべきであろう。「～んですから～」という言い方は，往々にして「あなたは知らないんですか」と非難の気持ちを相手に投げかける。

　文末表現で，話者の推測判断を示す「よう」「そう」「らしい」も問題になるものの１つだが，形容詞・形容動詞の語幹についた「そう」と「よう」の区別が特に難しい。次の例を参照していただきたい。

(1)　a．この試験は難しそうだ。
　　　b．この試験は難しいようだ。

(1a)は，例えば学生が試験問題をもらって，試験をする前に言う文だろう。つまり，「そう」は眼前にある対象を見て，それについての話者の視覚的印象を述べる表現である。「試験が小さい字で書いてあるから難しく見える」というだけで，事実難しいかどうかは問題になっていない。それに対して，(1b)は，例えば試験を監督している先生が学生の様子を見て言う文だろう。「よう」も観察に基づく場合が多いが，話者が責任を持って判断しているという感じが強い。

名詞句

　「その」と「あの」に誤用が目立つ。特に，「その」を使うべきところに「あの」を使う学生が多い。学生が「あの人」「あそこ」などと言うので，「えっ，私はその人を知らないのに」などと思うことがよくある。「あの」は話者と聞き手双方が知っていることを前提とするので，その点をよく教える必要がある。

　また，数詞と名詞との関係も問題になるものの１つである。まず，「みかんを３つ買った」と言うべきところを「*みかんを３つを買った」とか「*みかんの３つを買った」とか「３つのみかんを買った」などという間違いが多い。数量詞が名詞の前にくると，それがあるまとまりを持っている，一組になっているものという意味合いが強い。例えば「３冊の本」というと，３冊で一組になっているという意味が強いので，何冊買ったかを述べる場合は，「本を３冊買った」と数量詞を名詞のあとに持ってこなければならない。

動詞句

　自動詞・他動詞の区別，「する」と「なる」の使い分けなどに，やはり誤用が多い。また，英語との対比で特に気付くのは，英語で形容詞的な表現（[become] clear, [become] disappointed）が，日本語では，動詞表現になるものである。「はっきりする」で「*はっきりになる」とは言わない。

　英語に区別のない授受動詞の使い方，「〜てくる／〜ていく」などの使い方も注意をして教える必要がある。特に「くれる」の使い方は難しいが，「くれる」を教える際，疑問文では話者が聞き手の視点を取るので，「弟さんがくれたんですか」のように，やはり「くれる」になることをしっかり教えるべきであろう。

日本語の特徴の1つとして，感情を表わす形容詞と主語の人称との関係がある。例えば主語が一人称か二人称の場合，「欲しい」であるが，三人称の場合は「欲しがる」と言わなければならないと普通教える。そうすると，学生は，三人称主語の場合，どんな場合にも「がる」を使うので不自然な文がでてくる。(1)はその例である。

(1)　A：太郎は，どうしてアルバイトをしているんですか。

B：$\begin{cases} \text{a．車が欲しいから，} \\ \text{b．}^*\text{車を欲しがっているから，} \end{cases}$ アルバイトをしているんです。

原則として，「がる」は感情がそぶりに現われ，それを外から観察しているという意味合いがあるので，(1B)のように，話者が「太郎の立場に立って」ものを言っている場合には不適当である。

　その他，動詞の否定形の問題，例えば「ないで」なのか「なくて」なのか，「食べないでいる」なのか「食べていない」なのか等々，問題はいろいろあるが，詳しいことは本文を見ていただきたいと思う。

A STUDENTS' GUIDE TO
JAPANESE GRAMMAR

TEMPORAL AND RELATED EXPRESSIONS

1. *AIDA NI* vs. *UCHI NI*

Both *uchi ni* and *aida ni* indicate a certain time span during which an action occurs.

(1) a. アメリカにいるうちに
Amerika ni iru uchi ni 一度ワシントンへ行きたい。
b. アメリカにいる間に *ichido Washinton e ikitai.*
Amerika ni iru aida ni
'While we are in America, I would like to visit Washington.'

(2) a. 子供が寝ているうちに
Kodomo ga nete iru uchi ni 勉強した。
b. 子供が寝ている間に *benkyoo shita.*
Kodomo ga nete iru aida ni
'While the children were asleep, I studied.'

Aida is a noun which indicates a period between two points in time (e.g., *ichi ji to ni ji no aida* 'between one and two o'clock') and, as such, focuses on that period of time. *Uchi* is a noun which means 'inside, within', in contrast with *soto*, 'outside'.

This basic difference between *aida* and *uchi* also applies to cases like (1) and (2), where *aida* and *uchi* introduce a sentence. *Uchi ni* entails an implicit contrast with what comes after it, which, in most cases, is the end of a state described in the *uchi ni* clause. So, in (1a), the state of being in America is viewed in contrast to the *end* of this state, giving rise to a sense of urgency——i.e., "while we are still in America; before our stay is over." Similarly (2a) has a connotation of "studying before the children wake up; before it becomes impossible to study." Such sense of urgency is lacking with *aida ni*. *Aida ni* is more objective and simply focuses on what will/did happen during a certain period of time.

Observe the following sentences. ([*] indicates that the sentence is ungrammatical or unacceptable. [?] indicates that the sentence is unnatural or awkward.)

(3) a. 冷たいうちに飲んで下さい。
     Tsumetai uchi ni nonde kudasai.
   b. *冷たい間に飲んで下さい。
     **Tsumetai aida ni nonde kudasai.*
     'Please drink it while it is still cool.'

The whole point of uttering (3) is to suggest that someone drink before the drink gets lukewarm——before the state of "being cool" ends. Hence, *uchi ni* should be used in this situation.

There are cases, however, where *uchi ni* does not carry the sense of urgency evidenced in the above examples.

(4) 考えているうちにだんだん分かってきた。
   Kangaete iru uchi ni dandan wakatte kita.
   'While I thought about it, it gradually became clear.'
(5) 歩いているうちにかなり暗くなってきた。
   Aruite iru uchi ni kanari kuraku natte kita.
   'It became dark while we were walking.'
(6) 毎日練習しているうちに話せるようになってきた。
   Mainichi renshuu shite iru uchi ni hanaseru yoo ni natte kita.
   'While I practiced every day, I became able to speak.'

Notice that, in sentences (1)-(3), the main actions (e.g., going to

4

Washington) are controllable, while, in sentences (4)-(6), the main events (e.g., becoming clear) are beyond the person's control. In this latter case, *uchi ni* does not carry a sense of urgency, but simply focuses on the *change* which takes place.

> **BIBLIOGRAPHY**
> Kuno (1973), Terakura (1985), Backhouse & Quackenbush (1979), Kunihiro (1982)

2. *AIDA (NI)* vs. *TOKI (NI)*

Both *aida* and *toki* can indicate a period of time during which some action occurs, as in the following examples.

(1) 御飯を食べている　a. 間に　三度も電話がかかってき
　　　　　　　　　　　b. 時に　た。

　　　Gohan o tabete iru ｛ a. *aida ni* ｝ *sando mo denwa ga*
　　　　　　　　　　　　　 ｛ b. *toki ni* ｝

　　　kakatte kita.

'When I was eating dinner, the phone rang three times.'

(2) a. 日本にいる間に
　　　 Nihon ni iru aida ni ｜ いい友達ができました。
　　b. 日本にいる時 ｜ *ii tomodachi ga dekimashita.*
　　　 Nihon ni iru toki ｜

'When I was in Japan I made some good friends.'

In a word, *aida ni* indicates "during the time which" and *toki ni*, "at the time which." The difference between *aida ni* and *toki ni* is somewhat like "zooming in" vs. a "telescopic" photo in picture taking. With *aida ni*, the speaker zooms in to the designated time period and sees it from within, while, when *toki ni* is used, the speaker has telescopic view of the same time period and sees it from outside as a simple "point" in time.

Hence, when the speaker is involved in that time period and cannot have a telescopic view of it, *aida ni* but not *toki* is acceptable.

(3) 今子供が寝ているから，

Ima kodomo ga nete iru kara,

    a.   子供が寝ている間に勉強しよう。

        kodomo ga nete iru aida ni benkyoo shiyoo.

    b. *?子供が寝ている時勉強しよう。

        ?kodomo ga nete iru toki benkyoo shiyoo.

            'Since the child is asleep right now, I will study while (he) is sleeping.'

Suppose the child has just gone to sleep. In such a situation, the speaker is situated right in the time period of the child's sleeping. Here, *aida ni* should be used. If, however, the speaker is talking about what she would do the next day, both *aida ni* and *toki ni* are fine.

Similarly, when the actual change within a particular time period is emphasized, *aida ni* should be used.

(4) 仕事に夢中になっている $\left\{ \begin{matrix} 間に \\ *時 \end{matrix} \right\}$ 外は暗くなっていた。

  Shigoto ni muchuu ni natte iru $\left\{ \begin{matrix} aida\ ni \\ *toki \end{matrix} \right\}$ *soto wa*

  kuraku natte ita.

  'When I was absorbed in my work, it became dark outside.'

(5) 少し $\left\{ \begin{matrix} 見ない間に \\ ??見ない時に \end{matrix} \right\}$ ずいぶん大きくなりました。

  Sukoshi $\left\{ \begin{matrix} minai\ aida\ ni \\ ??minai\ toki\ ni \end{matrix} \right\}$ *zuibun ookiku narimashita.*

'The child has grown a lot while I haven't seen him.'

BIBLIOGRAPHY
Kunihiro (1982)

3. *MAE NI* vs. *NAI UCHI NI*

Expressions such as *mae ni* and *nai uchi ni* are both equivalent to English 'before.' (1) is an example.

(1) a. 寒くなる前にピクニックをしよう。
    Samuku naru mae ni pikunikku o shiyoo.
  b. 寒くならないうちにピクニックをしよう。
    Samuku naranai uchi ni pikunikku o shiyoo.
    'Let's have a picnic before it gets cold.'

First, in [X *mae ni/nai uchi ni* Y], if X represents an event which can be controlled by (i. e., can be brought about by the will of) the subject of Y, *mae ni* should be used.

(2) 車を $\left\{ \begin{array}{l} 買う前に \\ {}^*買わないうちに \end{array} \right\}$ よく調べましょう。

  Kuruma o $\left\{ \begin{array}{l} kau\ mae\ ni \\ {}^*kawanai\ uchi\ ni \end{array} \right\}$ yoku shirabemashoo.

  'Let's check the car over before we buy it.'

(3) 日本へ $\left\{ \begin{array}{l} 行く前に \\ {}^*行かないうちに \end{array} \right\}$ 日本語を勉強した。

  Nihon e $\left\{ \begin{array}{l} iku\ mae\ ni \\ {}^*ikanai\ uchi\ ni \end{array} \right\}$ nihongo o benkyoo shita.

  'I studied Japanese before I went to Japan.'

In (2) and (3), the subject of Y can bring about X by his own volition.

Here, *nai uchi ni* is inappropriate.

Second, if X represents an event which is not under the control of the subject of Y, then, both *mae ni* and *nai uchi ni* can be used.

(4)　a．暗くなる前に帰ろう。
　　　　Kuraku naru mae ni kaeroo.
　　　b．暗くならないうちに帰ろう。
　　　　Kuraku naranai uchi ni kaeroo.
　　　　'Let's go home before it gets dark.'

(5)　a．しかられる前にやめなさい。
　　　　Shikarareru mae ni yamenasai.
　　　b．しかられないうちにやめなさい。
　　　　Shikararenai uchi ni yamenasai.
　　　　'Stop it before you get scolded.'

In (4) and (5), X—i.e., 'getting dark' and 'being scolded'—is normally beyond one's control. In such cases, there are still some differences between *mae ni* and *nai uchi ni*.

When *mae ni* is used, the focus is on the *temporal sequence* between the two events. In (4), the sequence is between "getting dark" and "going home," and the speaker suggests "going home" *before* as opposed to *after* "it gets dark". In (5a), the speaker knows that the hearer is going to get scolded if he keeps up what he is doing and says to stop *before*, *not after*, he gets scolded.

Since a temporal sequence obtains between two definite events (events which are certain to happen), if X is an event which the speaker is not certain will happen or not, *mae ni* is inappropriate.

(6)　a．[?]雨が降る前に帰ろう。
　　　　[?]*Ame ga furu mae ni kaeroo.*
　　　　'Let's go home before it rains.'
　　　b．雨が降る前に帰った。
　　　　Ame ga furu mae ni kaetta.

'I went home before it rained.'

One is never completely certain if it will rain or not, and hence, *mae ni* is awkward in (6a). Of course, if the sentence is in the past tense, we are talking of a definite event, and hence *mae ni* is fine in (6b).

Nai uchi ni, on the other hand, carries a certain negative implication—i.e., one hopes X does not get realized; one does Y so as to prevent an unfavorable consequence. Furthermore, there is a sense of urgency that one should do something *before it is too late*. So, in (4b), the focus is on the speaker's negative attitude toward having to go home in the dark. (4b) says "Let's go home now so as *not* to have to face the unfavorable consequence of having to walk in the dark." (5b) says "Quit it so as *not* to be scolded." If *mae ni* is used, the statements are much more objective. Consider the following sentences.

(7) a. 二十歳になる前に結婚した。
    Hatachi ni naru mae ni kekkon shita.
  b. 二十歳にならないうちに結婚した。
    Hatachi ni naranai uchi ni kekkon shita.
    '(He/She) got married before (he/she) was twenty.'

(7a) is an objective statement about when he/she got married—i. e., it was before he/she became twenty, not after. (7b), on the other hand, carries the speaker's negative evaluation—one's disapproval that he/she got married so early.

The following sentences cannot be interpreted as temporal, and hence *mae ni* is inappropriate.

(8) a. ^{??}忘れる前に書いておこう。
    ^{??}*Wasureru mae ni kaite okoo.*
  b. 忘れないうちに書いておこう。
    Wasurenai uchi ni kaite okoo.
    'I will write it down before I forget it.'

(9)　a．　??さめる前に召しあがって下さい。

　　　　??*Sameru mae ni meshiagatte kudasai.*

　　b．　さめないうちに召しあがって下さい。

　　　　Samenai uchi ni meshiagatte kudasai.

　　　　'Please help yourself before it gets cold.'

The question here is not temporal——i.e., it is strange to talk of writing before as opposed to after one forgets, since one cannot write it down once it is forgotten. What the speaker is saying in (8) is that one should write so as *not* to forget, and hence *nai uchi ni* should be used. Similarly, (9b) says that one should eat now so the food does *not* get cold.

> **BIBLIOGRAPHY**
> Kuno (1973), Terakura (1985)

4. *TA* vs. *RU*

So called tense markers in Japanese (*-ru/-u* and *-ta*) indicate a *time-relationship* between two events/states rather than an absolute time. While the English past tense indicates that an event or a state occurred at some point in the past, *ta* in Japanese merely indicates that an event is completed before or "earlier than" some other event. Some other event could be either the moment of speech or another event. (Miura 1974 : 95–96.)

(1)　a．　きのう学校へ来た。

　　　　Kinoo gakkoo e ki-ta.

　　　　'(I) came to school yesterday.'

　　b．　あした朝学校へ来た人にあげます。

　　　　Ashita asa gakkoo e ki-ta hito ni agemasu.

'(I) will give it to the people who come to school tomorrow
morning.'

In (1a), *ta* indicates that someone's coming to school took place
"earlier than" the moment of speech. This usage corresponds to that
of English past tense. In (1b), however, someone's coming to school
has not happened yet——it will happen in the future. *Ta* is used here
to indicate that "coming to school" will be completed before the
action of "giving." This usage corresponds to the English "perfective" tense.

Ru, on the other hand, indicates that an event or a state is "not
completed" or "not earlier than" either the moment of speech or
another event/state. [*Ru* is used here as a general term referring to
both *-ru* and *-u* forms.]

    (2)   a. あした学校へ行く。
               Ashita gakkoo e ik-u.
               'I will go to school tomorrow.'
        b. きのう学校へ行く人を見た。
               Kinoo gakkoo e ik-u hito o mi-ta.
               'Yesterday I saw people who were going to school.'
        c. あそこに人がいる。
               Asoko ni hito ga i-ru.
               'There are people over there.'
        d. きのう着物を着ている人に会った。
               Kinoo kimono o kite i-ru hito ni at-ta.
               'Yesterday I met a person who had a kimono on.'

In (2a), *ru* indicates that an action of going to school has not
happened at the moment of uttering this sentence——i.e., "not earlier
than the moment of speech." (2b) indicates that an action of someone's going to school was not completed at the time the speaker saw
these people——i.e., "not earlier than" the main event of "seeing."

Sentences (2c) and (2d) contain stative verbs such as *iru* and *kite iru*. When *ru* occurs with stative verbs, "not earlier than" should be interpreted as "simultaneous." Thus, in (2c), the state of someone's existence is simultaneous with the moment of speech. In (2d), the person's having a kimono on was simultaneous with the speaker's meeting with this person.

The use of *ta* and *ru* in relative clauses can be illustrated schematically as follows. In the following, we will refer to a relative clause as Event A and the main clause as Event B. The diagram below represents the progression of time (from left to right). MS stands for the moment of speech (i.e., NOW), and the time events A and B occur relative to each other is plotted. Our primary concern here is what form Event A takes.

A. When the main clause (=Event B) is in *ru*-form:

1. When Event A occurs after Event B:

```
           MS         Event B     Event A
  ─────────|───────────|───────────|─────────→
                                        ru
```

(3) 田中さんにあげるものを駅の前で買う。

    Tanaka-san ni ageru mono o eki no mae de kau.

             E/A   E/B

    'I will buy the thing I will be giving to Mr. Tanaka at the station.'

Ru should be used for Event A since Event A (=*ageru*) is not completed before Event B nor the moment of speech.

2. When Event A has not happened yet but will occur before Event B:

```
           MS         Event A     Event B
  ─────────|───────────|───────────|─────────→
                         ta (ex. 4 & 5)
                        (ru) (ex. 6)
```

(4) あした来た人にあげます。

Ashita kita hito ni agemasu.

E/A   E/B

'I will give it to those who (will have) come tomorrow.'

(5) 私は毎日母の作ったお弁当を食べる。

Watashi wa mainichi haha no tsukutta obentoo o taberu.

E/A   E/B

'Everyday I eat the lunch my mother prepares.'

Since the sentences focus on the completion of Event A *before* Event B, *ta* is preferred, although the events have not happened yet. (4) and (5) are examples. If, however, there are adverbs which will make it clear that Event A will take place after the moment of speech, as in (6), *ru* should be used.

(6) きょう勉強することもあしたのテストに出ます。

Kyoo benkyoo suru koto mo ashita no tesuto ni demasu.

E/A   E/B

'What we will study today will be on tomorrow's test.'

3. When Event A occurred in the past (i.e., before MS):

(7) きのう買った本を今日読みます。

Kinoo katta hon o kyoo yomimasu.

E/A   E/B

'Today I will read the book I bought yesterday.'

Ta should be used here since it was completed before the moment of speech.

B. When the main clause (= Event B) is in *ta*-form:

1. When Event A occurs before Event B:

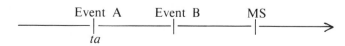

13

(8) きのうパーティーで会った男がさっきここへ来た。

Kinoo paatii de atta otoko ga sakki koko e kita.

       E/A   E/B

'The man whom I met at the party yesterday came here a while ago.'

2. When Event A occurs after Event B but before MS:

```
          Event B       Event A      MS
 ─────────┼─────────────┼────────────┼──────────→
                      ru  (ex. 9, 10)
                     (ta) (ex. 11)
```

(9) きのう田中さんの家へ行った。駅の前で田中さんにあげるものを買った。

Kinoo Tanaka san no uchi e itta. Eki no mae de Tanaka-san ni ageru mono o katta.

'I went to Tanaka's yesterday. I bought a gift I was going to give to Ms. Tanaka at the station.'

(10) きのうフットボールのゲームに行く人を大勢見かけた。

Kinoo futtobooru no geemu ni iku hito o oozei mikaketa.

'Yesterday I saw many people who were going to the football game.'

(11) さっきここにいた人はきのうもここへ来ました。

Sakki koko ni ita hito wa kinoo mo koko e kimashita.

'The person who was here a while ago came here yesterday also.'

In this case, Event A is completed before the moment of speech but not completed before Event B. Here, *ru* should be used if the focus is on non-completion of Event A in relation to Event B. In (9), the context makes it clear that the action of giving has already occurred. The action of giving, however, took place after the action of buying, and hence *ru* is used. If, however, there is an adverb such as *sakki* which makes it clear that Event A is related to the moment of speech, as in (11), *ta* should be used.

3. When Event A occurs after MS:

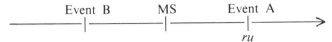

Event B   MS   Event A

ru

(12)　あした話をする人がさっきここへ来た。

Ashita hanashi o su<u>ru</u> hito ga sakki koko e ki-ta.

'The person who will be talking tomorrow came here a while ago.'

Here, *ru* should be used.

The cases which are clearly different from English are A-2 and B-2, and they require special attention. Compare the following sentences.

(13)　a. 日本へ行った人と話した。

Nihon e itta hito to hanashita.

'I talked to a person who had been to Japan.'

    b. 日本へ行く人と話した。

Nihon e iku hito to hanashita.

'I talked to a person who was going to Japan.'

Ta in (13a) signals "completion"—i.e., the person had already been to Japan when the speaker talked to him. *Ru* in (13b) indicates "non-completion"—i.e., the person was going to go to Japan at the time the speaker talked with him.

(14)　a. 田中さんにあげるものを買った。

Tanaka-san ni ageru mono o katta.

'I bought the thing I was going to give to Ms. Tanaka.'

    b. ʔ田中さんにあげたものを買った。

ʔ*Tanaka-san ni ageta mono o katta.*

'I bought the thing I had given to Ms. Tanaka.'

Since "giving" cannot precede "buying," *ta* is inappropriate in (14).

(15)　a. あした一番早く来た人にこれをあげて下さい。

Ashita ichiban hayaku kita hito ni kore o agete

kudasai.

'Please give this to the person who will have come the earliest tomorrow.'

b. [?]あした一番早く来る人にこれをあげて下さい。

  [?]*Ashita ichiban hayaku kuru hito ni kore o agete kudasai.*

  'Please give this to the person who is going to come the earliest tomorrow.'

Since "coming" has to happen before "giving," *ta* should be used. It seems that *ru* should also be appropriate here since the action of "coming" has not happened yet at the Moment of Speech. *Ru*, however, is strange in this context. Sentence (15b) says "please give this now to the person who is sure to come the earliest tomorrow."

A similar distinction holds for *ru* and *ta* in *toki*-clauses.

1. When Event A and Event B are simultaneous:

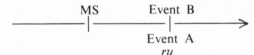

(16) バスを降りる時，注意しなさい。

  Basu o oriru toki, chuui shinasai.

    E/A   E/B

  'Be careful when you step out of the bus.'

2. When Event A happens before Event B but after MS:

(17) バスを降りた時，注意しなさい。

  Basu o orita toki, chuui shinasai.

    E/A   E/B

  'Be careful when (after) you get off the bus.'

Although Event A has not happened yet, *ta* is used since it will be completed before Event B.

3． When Event A and Event B are simultaneous, but happened before MS:

```
            Event B        MS
────────────┼─────────────┼────────→
            Event A
            ru (ex. 18, 19b, 20b)
            (ta) (ex. 19a, 20a)
```

(18) きのうバスを降りる時変な女の人を見た。

    Kinoo basu o oriru toki henna onna no hito o mita.

         E/A   E/B

    'Yesterday when I was getting off the bus, I saw a strange woman.'

Since Event A and Event B are simultaneous, *ru* should be used. If, however, Event A entails certain duration, *ta* can be used, as in (19) and (20). Here, however, the focus is on the completion of an event before the moment of speech.

(19) スミスさんはきのう御飯を｛ a．食べた / b．食べる ｝時，おはしを上手に使った。

    Sumisu-san wa kinoo gohan o ｛ a. tabe-ta / b. tabe-ru ｝ toki,

    ohashi o joozu ni tsukatta.

    'Mr. Smith used chopsticks very well when he ate yesterday.'

(20) スミスさんは日本に｛ a．住んでいた / b．住んでいる ｝時には日本語を話した。

    Sumisu-san wa nihon ni ｛ a. sunde ita / b. sunde iru ｝ toki ni wa ni-

    hongo o hanashita.

'Mr. Smith spoke Japanese when he lived in Japan.'

Since both Event A and Event B occurred at the same time, *ru* is also appropriate.

4. When Event A occurs before Event B and before MS:

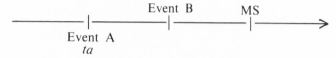

(21) きのうバスを降りた時，変な女の人を見た。

kinoo basu o orita toki, henna onna no hito o mita.

'I saw a strange woman when (after) I got off the bus.'

So, compare the following sentences.

(22) a. 日本へ行く時カメラを買った。

Nihon e iku toki kamera o katta.

'I bought a camera when I was going to Japan.'

b. 日本へ行った時カメラを買った。

Nihon e itta toki kamera o kat-ta.

'I bought a camera when (after) I went to Japan.'

(22a) means that the person bought a camera either just before going to Japan or on the way to Japan. (22b), on the other hand, means that he bought a camera after he got to Japan.

> **BIBLIOGRAPHY**
> Kuno (1973), Miura (1974), Nakau (1976), Soga (1983)

5. *TARA, NARA, TO* vs. *BA*

There are four conditionals in Japanese.

(1) a. 日本へ行ったら
   Nihon e it-tara

   b. 日本へ行くと   日本語が上手になります。
   Nihon e iku to   *nihongo ga joozu ni narimasu.*

   c. 日本へ行けば
   Nihon e ik-eba

$$S_1 \qquad\qquad\qquad S_2$$

'If you go to Japan, your Japanese will improve.'

   d. 日本へ行く（ん）なら日本語を勉強した方がいい。
   *Nihon e iku(n)nara nihongo o benkyoo shi-ta hoo ga
   ii.*

$$S_1 \qquad\qquad\qquad S_2$$

'If you are going to Japan, you had better study Japanese.'

Among these, *tara* and *to* have both a conditional (i.e., if) function and a temporal (i.e., when) function. Whether they are interpreted as a conditional or as a temporal depends on whether S_1 is certain to happen or not. Sentences (1a) and (1b), for example, can be uttered either when you know the addressee is going to Japan or when you don't know if he is going or not. In the former, *tara/to* is temporal. In the latter case, they are conditional.

(2) a. 日が暮れたら、帰りましょう。
   Hi ga kure-tara, kaerimashoo.
   'When it gets dark, let's go home.'

   b. 十月になると、寒くなります。
   Juugatsu ni naru to, samuku narimasu.
   'When it gets to be October, it becomes cold.'

(3) a. 雨が降ったら、ピクニックをやめましょう。
   Ame ga fut-tara, pikunikku o yamemashoo.
   'If it rains, let's not have a picnic.'

   b. 雨が降ると、ピクニックができません。
   Ame ga furu to, pikunikku ga dekimasen.

'If it rains, we cannot have a picnic.'

In a normal situation, (2) would be interpreted as temporal since you know that S_1 is certain to happen. Sentence (3) would be most likely interpreted as conditional since you don't know for sure if it is going to rain or not.

Of the four conditionals, *tara* has the broadest range of usage, and can be safely used in most cases. However, there are some clear differences among these forms.

1) *To* represents a habitual or logical antecedent-consequent relationship (Kuno 1973 : 193). It is used to describe a general truth, a habitual action and the like.

(4) 春になると，あたたかくなります。
　　 Haru ni naru to, atatakaku narimasu.
　　 'When spring comes, it becomes warm.'

(5) 夜コーヒーを飲むと，寝られません。
　　 Yoru koohii o nomu to, neraremasen.
　　 'If I drink coffee at night, I cannot go to sleep.'

Both (4) and (5) describe a situation such that whenever S_1 occurs, then S_2 will always occur. It is a universal truth that it becomes warm when spring comes. (5) also describes a habitual truth.

2) *Tara* emphasizes the fact that S_2 happens after S_1 is completed.

(6) 田中さんが来たら，私は帰ります。
　　 Tanaka-san ga ki-tara, watashi wa kaerimasu.
　　 'If/when Mr. Tanaka comes, I will go home.'

"My" going home will take place *after* Tanaka's coming.

3) *Nara* asserts S_1 to be true. Normally, S_1 is what someone (the hearer) has just said. In contrast to *tara*, in $[S_1$ *nara* $S_2]$, S_2 cannot happen after S_1 is completed, if S_1 has not happened yet. (Kuno

1973：176.)

(7)　A：日本へ行きます。

　　　Nihon e ikimasu.

　　B：a．日本へ行くんなら，JAL で行きなさい。

　　　　　Nihon e iku n nara, JAL de ikinasai.

　　　　　'If you are going to Japan (as you say you are), go by JAL.'

　　　b．日本へ $\left\{ \begin{array}{l} {}^*行くんなら， \\ 行ったら， \end{array} \right\}$ 日本語が上手になるでしょう。

　　　　　Nihon e $\left\{ \begin{array}{l} {}^*iku\ n\ nara, \\ it\text{-}tara, \end{array} \right\}$ *nihongo ga joozu ni*

　　　　　naru deshoo.

　　　　　'If you are going to Japan, your Japanese will get better.'

In (7Ba), *nara* asserts what A said. In (7Ba), *nara*, moreover, is fine because S_2——going by JAL——occurs simultaneously with S_1. If S_2, however, happens after S_1 is completed (as in (7Bb)), *tara* has to be used.

If S_1 has already taken place, as in (8), there is no such restriction on the temporal sequencing between S_1 and S_2.

(8)　A：田中さんが来ましたよ。

　　　Tanaka-san ga kimashita yo.

　　　'Mr. Tanaka came.'

　　B：田中さんが来たんなら，私は帰ります。

　　　Tanaka-san ga kita n nara, watashi wa kaerimasu.

　　　'If Mr. Tanaka has come (as you say he has), I am going home.'

In (8B), the speaker says he will go home if someone's assertion that

Tanaka has come is indeed true. Here, "my" going will take place after Tanaka's coming.

4) *Ba* gives a necessary condition for S_2. It has the connotation of 'if only'.

(9) A：どうやったら日本語が上手になるでしょうか。
Doo yattara nihongo ga joozu ni naru deshoo ka ?
'How can I improve my Japanese ?'

B：日本へ行けば上手になりますよ。
Nihon e ik-eba joozu ni narimasu yo.
'If you go to Japan, you will improve your Japanese.'

Speaker A wants to improve his Japanese, and the use of *ba* implies "all you have to do is to go to Japan."

Compare the following sentences.

(10) a . あなたが読んだら、私も読みます。
Anata ga yon-dara, watashi mo yomimasu.
b . あなたが読むんなら、私も読みます。
Anata ga yomu n nara, watashi mo yomimasu.
c . あなたが読めば、私も読みます。
Anata ga yom-eba, watashi mo yomimasu.
d . *あなたが読むと、私も読みます。
* *Anata ga yomu to, watashi mo yomimasu.*

Sentence (10a) emphasizes the completion of S_1 before S_2 happens, and hence implies that "your" reading precedes "my" reading. (10b) would be used when the hearer says he is going to read the book, and the speaker asserts "if it is indeed the case that you are going to read the book, I will read it also." What is important here is the assertion and "my" reading could occur either before or after "your" reading. (10c) says that the only way "I" will read is if "you" read. *To* is inappropriate in (10) since S_2 represents the speaker's intention. If the subject of S_2 is someone else, however, the sentence is perfectly acceptable—*"Anata ga yomu to Tanaka-san mo yomimasu."*

(11)   a. くすりを飲んだら，
        Kusuri o non-dara,

      b. くすりを飲むと，
        Kusuri o nomu to,   直ります。

      c. くすりを飲めば，   *naorimasu.*
        Kusuri o nom-eba,

      d. *くすりを飲むなら，
        *Kusuri o nomu nara,

(11a) focuses on the temporal sequence——"If you take the medicine, then you will get better." (11b) would be used in the same situation with (11a). (11b), however, presents the proposition as a universal truth——getting better is a logical or natural consequence of taking medicine. (11c) implies that "all one has to do to get better is to take medicine." *Nara* is inappropriate here because S_2 depends on the future realization of S_1. Of course, if S_1 is in the past tense as in *"Kusuri o nonda n nara, naorimasu"*, the sentence is fine and means "If you have taken the medicine (as you say), then you will get better."

The following is another example of *tara* vs. *nara*.

(12)   a. 日本語を勉強したら，日本へ行きなさい。
        Nihongo o benkyoo shi-tara, nihon e ikinasai.
        'After you study Japanese, go to Japan.'

      b. 日本語を勉強するんなら，日本へ行きなさい。
        Nihongo o benkyoo suru n nara, nihon e ikinasai.
        'If you are going to study Japanese (as you say you are), go
        to Japan.'

In (12a), the speaker is advising the hearer to go to Japan after he studies Japanese. In (12b), on the other hand, the speaker is

23

advising the hearer to go to Japan and study Japanese in Japan.

Above we have examined sentences which contain action verbs in S_1. Semantic differences described above are not as pronounced when S_1 represents a state.

(13) a. おもしろかったら、
    Omoshirokattara,

  b. おもしろいと、
    Omoshiroi to,   売れます。

  c. おもしろければ、 *uremasu.*
    Omoshirokereba,

  d. おもしろいなら、
    Omoshiroi nara,

  'If it's interesting, it will sell.'

(14) a. 静かだったら、
    Shizuka dattara,

  b. 静かだと、   勉強できます。
    Shizuka da to, *benkyoo dekimasu.*

  c. 静かなら、
    Shizuka nara,

  'If it is quiet, I can study.'

In (13) and (14), they all give a condition under which one buys or one can study.

Some of these conditionals, moreover, do not allow subjective expressions to occur in S_2. Subjective expressions are request, suggestion, invitation and the like.

(15) a. 日本語を勉強したら、日本へ行きなさい。
    Nihongo o benkyoo shitara, nihon e ikinasai.

  b. 日本語を勉強するんなら、日本へ行きなさい。
    Nihongo o benkyoo suru n nara, nihon e ikinasai.

  c. *日本語を勉強すると、日本へ行きなさい。

Nihongo o benkyoo suru to, nihon e ikinasai.

d.　*日本語を勉強すれば，日本へ行きなさい。

Nihongo o benkyoo sureba, nihon e ikinasai.

'If you study Japanese, go to Japan.'

(16)　a.　安かったら買いなさい。

Yasukattara kainasai.

b.　安いんなら買いなさい。

Yasui n nara kainasai.

c.　安ければ買いなさい。

Yasukereba kainasai.

d.　*安いと買いなさい。

Yasui to kainasai.

'If it is cheap, buy it.'

To does not allow subjective expressions to occur in S_2. *Ba* allows subjective expressions in S_2 when S_1 represents a state, but not when S_1 is an action.

BIBLIOGRAPHY

Akatsuka (1985), Alfonso (1966), Kuno (1973), McGloin (1976-77)

6. *TARA* vs. *TO* (past)

When the main sentence is in the past tense, both *tara* and *to* can be used with the sense of 'when.'

(1)　a.　外へ出たら，雨が降っていた。

Soto e detara, ame ga futte ita.

b.　外へ出ると，雨が降っていた。

Soto e deru to, ame ga futte ita.

'When I went out, it was raining.'

Tara and *to*, however, are not always interchangeable. Observe the following sentences.

(2)　a.　＊太郎は家へ帰ったら，御飯を作った。

   ＊*Taroo wa uchi e kaettara, gohan o tsukutta.*

  b.　太郎は家へ帰ると，御飯を作った。

   Taroo wa uchi e kaeru to, gohan o tsukutta.

   'When he went home, Taroo cooked dinner.'

(3)　a.　＊田中はいすにすわったら，話をはじめた。

   ＊*Tanaka wa isu ni suwattara, hanashi o hajimeta.*

  b.　田中はいすにすわると，話をはじめた。

   Tanaka wa isu ni suwaru to, hanashi o hajimeta.

   'When he sat down, Tanaka began to talk.'

With *tara*, the sequence of two actions (S_1 and S_2) cannot be something which can be controlled by the subject (Kuno 1973 : 193). In (2), the actions of going home and preparing a meal are both under the volition of the subject. In (3), sitting on a chair and talking are both controlled by the will of the subject. Hence, *tara* is unacceptable in (2) and (3). The most natural way of expressing such a sequence is the use of the *te*-form, as in (4) and (5).

(4)　太郎は家へ帰って，御飯を作った。

  Taroo wa uchi e kaette, gohan o tsukutta.

  'Taroo went home and cooked dinner.'

(5)　田中はいすにすわって話をはじめた。

  Tanaka wa isu ni suwatte hanashi o hajimeta.

  'Tanaka sat down and started to talk.'

To, on the other hand, does allow S_1 and S_2 to be controlled by the subject. When *to* is used, however, the event must be an objective event which can be observed by the speaker. In (2) and (3), the

speaker can objectively report these events since they involve someone other than the speaker.   If, however, the speaker himself/herself
is involved as in (6),

(6) 私はその日，家へ帰ると，御飯を作った。
Watashi wa sono hi, uchi e kaeru to, gohan o tsukutta.
'That day, when I went home, I made dinner.'

it has to be in a special story-telling context where the speaker can
detach himself/herself and report on the event objectively.   Without
such a story-telling flavor, sentence (6) would be odd and the *-te*
form should be used.

BIBLIOGRAPHY
Kuno (1973)

7. TE IRU / TE ITA vs. RU/TA

The meaning of V-*te iru* can be classified into at least four types.

(A)   Action in Progress

(1) テニスをしています。
Tenisu o shite imasu.
'(I) am playing tennis.'

(2) 雨が降っています。
Ame ga futte imasu.
'It is raining.'

(B)   State in Effect (a state which resulted from an action.)

(3) セーターを着ています。
Seetaa o kite imasu.

'(I) have a sweater on.'

(4) 結婚しています。

Kekkon shite imasu.

'(I) am married.'

(C) Experience

(5) その本は何年も前に読んでいる。

Sono hon wa nan-nen mo mae ni yonde iru.

'I read that book many years ago.'

(6) 田中さんは三冊本を書いている。

Tanaka-san wa sansatsu hon o kaite iru.

'Mr. Tanaka has written three books.'

(D) Habitual Action

(7) 会社に勤めています。

Kaisha ni tsutomete imasu.

'(I) am employed by a company.'

(8) このごろ毎日ランゲージ・ラボへ行っている。

Konogoro mainichi rangeeji rabo e itte iru.

'I am going to the language lab every day these days.'

Of these, (A) and (B) are the most essential. Verbs which indicate an activity such as 'to read', 'to play', 'to walk', etc. belong to the (A)-type. Verbs which belong to the (B)-type——i.e., verbs whose *te iru* forms indicate a "resulting state" are: (1) motion verbs (*iku, kuru, kaeru,* etc.), (2) verbs of wearing (*kiru, kaburu, haku,* etc.), and (3) verbs such as *kekkonsuru, shinu, wasureru, hairu, aku,* etc., which are viewed as an "instantaneous" action, for which you cannot specify a beginning point and an end point. For instance, you cannot talk about someone's beginning to get married (*kekkon-shi-hajimeta) or finishing getting married (*kekkon-shi-owatta).

Following are some more examples of type (B).

(9)   スミスさんは日本へ行っています。

　　　Sumisu-san wa nihon e itte imasu.

　　　'Mr. Smith has gone to Japan and is there now.'

(10)   犬が死んでいます。

　　　Inu ga shinde imasu.

　　　'There is a dead dog.'

(11)   帽子をかぶっています。

　　　Booshi o kabutte imasu.

　　　'(He) has a hat on.'

Sentence (9a) does not indicate that someone is in the process of going to Japan. It indicates that Smith is in Japan as a result of having gone to Japan. (10) indicates a state that a dog is dead. (11) generally does not mean that someone is in the process of putting a hat on, but means that someone has a hat on.

Note also that the verbs *sumu* and *motsu* should be used in the *te iru* form when they indicate someone's current state of residence and possession, respectively.

(12)   a. 東京に住んでいます。

　　　　　Tookyoo ni sunde imasu.

　　　　　'(I) live in Tokyo.'

　　　b. 日本語の辞書を持っています。

　　　　　Nihongo no jisho o motte imasu.

　　　　　'I have a Japanese dictionary.'

"Activity" verbs which generally indicate "action in progress" in the *te iru* form can indicate "resulting state" or "experience" if the goal or the final accomplishment is focused.

(13)   a. 山をのぼっている。

　　　　　Yama o nobotte iru.

　　　　　'(He) is climbing the mountain.'

　　　b. 山にのぼっている。

Yama ni nobotte iru.

'(He) has climbed (and is on top of) the mountain.'

(14) a. あの人はとなりの部屋で本を読んでいる。

Ano hito wa tonari no heya de hon o yonde iru.

'He is reading a book in the next room.'

b. その本は何年も前に読んでいる。

Sono hon wa nan-nen mo mae ni yonde iru.

'I have read that book many years ago.'

The use of *o* in (13a) indicates that in (13a) the process of climbing the mountain is focused. The particle *ni* in (13b), however, puts the focus on the final accomplishment of climbing the mountain, and hence the "resulting state" meaning of *te iru*. While (14a) gives a normal "action in progress" interpretation, (14b) emphasizes the accomplishment of having read the book, and hence (14b) gives an experiential reading.

For those verbs which have morphologically marked transitive vs. intransitive verb forms such as *aku/akeru*, *tsuku/tsukeru*, etc., *te iru* indicates "action in progress" when used with a transitive form and "state in effect" when used with an intransitive form.

(15) a. 窓をあけています。

Mado o akete imasu.

'I am opening the window.'

b. 窓があいています。

Mado ga aite imasu.

'The door is open.'

(16) a. ビールをひやしています。

Biiru o hiyashite imasu.

'I am cooling the beer.'

b. ビールがひえています。

Biiru ga hiete imasu.

'The beer is chilled.'

(15a) and (16a) indicate "action in progress." (15b) and (16b) indicate current states.

One should be careful in distinguishing *ru/ta* forms from *te iru* forms, especially with verbs whose *te iru* form indicates "resulting state." Observe the following.

(17) a . 来年 $\left\{ \begin{array}{l} 結婚するでしょう。 \\ *結婚しているでしょう。 \end{array} \right\}$

Rainen $\left\{ \begin{array}{l} kekkon\ suru\ deshoo. \\ *kekkon\ shite\ iru\ deshoo. \end{array} \right\}$

'I will be married next year.'

b . 結婚 $\left\{ \begin{array}{l} したことがありますか。 \\ *していたことがありますか。 \end{array} \right\}$

Kekkon $\left\{ \begin{array}{l} shita\ koto\ ga\ arimasu\ ka? \\ *shite\ ita\ koto\ ga\ arimasu\ ka? \end{array} \right\}$

'Have you ever been married?'

c . 二年前まで $\left\{ \begin{array}{l} 結婚していました。 \\ *結婚しました。 \end{array} \right\}$

Ninen mae made $\left\{ \begin{array}{l} kekkon\ shite\ imashita. \\ *kekkon\ shimashita. \end{array} \right\}$

'I had been married until two years ago.'

d . あの二人が $\left\{ \begin{array}{l} 結婚したら \\ 結婚していたら \end{array} \right\}$ 知らせて下さい。

Ano futari ga $\left\{ \begin{array}{l} kekkon\ shitara \\ kekkon\ shite\ itara \end{array} \right\}$ *shirasete*

kudasai.

'If those two $\left\{ \begin{array}{l} \text{get married,} \\ \text{are married,} \end{array} \right\}$ please let me know.'

(18) a . (五時になると)暗くなることを知りませんでした。

(*Goji ni naru to*) *kuraku naru koto o shirimasen deshita.*

'I did not know that it gets dark (at five o'clock).'

b. 外が暗くなっていることを知りませんでした。

Soto ga kuraku natte iru koto o shirimasen deshita.

'I did not know that it had gotten dark outside.'

In (17b), *koto ga aru* puts an emphasis on the action of getting married. In (17c), the state of being married is focused.

Verbs *omou* and *kangaeru* should be used in *te iru* form when the subject is a third person, as in (19b).

(19) a. 私はそんな人はいないと思います。

Watashi wa sonna hito wa inai to omoimasu.

'I think there is no such person.'

b. 田中さんはそんな人はいないと { 思っています。 / *思います。 }

Tanaka-san wa sonna hito wa inai to
{ *omotte imasu.* / **omoimasu.* }

'Mr. Tanaka thinks there is no such person.'

However, in many embedded clauses, the *ta* form is fine, as in (20).

(20) a. 田中さんは，自分が天才だと思ったことがあるそうです。

Tanaka-san wa jibun ga tensai da to omotta koto ga aru soo desu.

'I hear Mr. Tanaka has thought that he is a genius.'

b. A：田中さんはどうしてそんな事をしたんでしょうか。

Tanaka-san wa dooshite sonna koto o shita n deshoo ka?

'Why did Mr. Tanaka do such a thing?'

B：自分が天才だと { 思っていた / 思った } からでしょう。

$$\textit{Jibun ga tensai da to} \left\{ \begin{array}{l} \textit{omotte ita} \\ \textit{omotta} \end{array} \right\} \textit{kara deshoo.}$$

'It's because $\left\{ \begin{array}{l} \text{he had been thinking that} \\ \text{he thought that} \end{array} \right\}$ he was a

genius.'

In (20b), the use of *ta* vs. *te ita* results in meaning differences. *Te ita* here is perfective (i.e., had been thinking), while *ta* refers to a past action of thinking at a particular moment.

8. *TE IRU* vs. *TE ARU*

Te aru is used only with transitive verbs and indicates "state in effect", as in (1) and (2).

(1) ビールがひやしてあります。
   Biiru ga hiyashite arimasu.
   'The beer has been chilled.'

(2) お茶が入れてあります。
   Ocha ga irete arimasu.
   'Tea has been served.'

There are some differences between V -*te iru* and V -*te aru* when they indicate "state in effect." V -*te aru* implies that someone did an action for *some purpose*. No such intention is implied in V -*te iru*.

(3) a. 窓があけてあります。
      Mado ga akete arimasu.
      'The window has been opened.'

   b. 窓があいています。
      Mado ga aite imasu.

'The window is open.'

Sentence (3a) is used when the window has been opened deliberately for some purpose such as to let fresh air come in. In a situation where one comes back to the house and discovers that the window is open and does not know who did it or why, (3b) should be used.

(4)   a. ビールがひやしてあります。

          Biiru ga hiyashite arimasu.

          'The beer has been chilled.'

     b. ビールがひえています。

          Biiru ga hiete imasu.

          'The beer is chilled / There is some cold beer.'

Sentence (4a) could be used when one is having a party and tells a friend that beer has been chilled and is ready to go. A wife, on her husband's return, on the other hand, could utter either (4a) or (4b). In such a case, the difference is a matter of focus. (4a) would imply that the chilling beer was especially done for him. (4b), on the other hand, states the fact matter-of-factly.

9. (*te*) *KURU* vs. (*te*) *IKU*

Motion verbs *kuru* 'to come' and *iku* 'to go' are often used as auxiliary verbs to indicate how a certain event/action relates to the speaker in space or in time. It is well known that in sentences such as (1),

(1)   a. 食べて来ました。

          Tabete kimashita.

          'I have eaten (before I came).'

     b. 食べて行きました。

Tabete ikimashita.
'I ate (before I went).'

kuru indicates the spacial movement toward the speaker (i.e., the speaker came to where he is after eating); *iku* indicates a spacial movement away from the speaker (i.e., the speaker moved away from where he was after eating.) It is extremely important that *kuru* and *iku* are used here since the verb itself (i.e., *taberu*) does not relate the action to the immediate presence of the speaker.

Kuru and *iku* are also used with verbs of process, transition or change, and indicate how a certain change relates to the speaker in time. *Kuru* indicates that a certain change has been taking place toward the speaker in a temporal sense (i.e., "up to now"). *Iku* indicates that a change / process will continue away from the speaker in a temporal sense (i.e., "from now on.") This can be illustrated by (2).

(2)

	te kuru	*te iku*	
past		present	future

a. みるみる変わってきました。
   Mirumiru kawatte kimashita.
   'It has begun to change rapidly.'
b. どんどん変わっていくでしょう。
   Dondon kawatte iku deshoo.
   'It will continue to change rapidly.'

In (2a), the speaker is looking back at the change——the change has been taking place. In (2b), the change will take place.

In this temporal usage of *kuru*, there are two basic usages: "continuation" and "inception."

(3) a. 今までずっと我慢してきました。
     Ima made zutto gamanshite kimashita.

'I have continued to put up (with it) up until now.'

b. 一生懸命生きてきました。

Isshookenmei ikite kimashita.

'I have lived to my utmost capacity up until now.'

(4) a. 寒くなってきました。

Samuku natte kimashita.

'It's beginning to get cold.'

b. このごろ太ってきましたね。

Konogoro futotte kimashita ne.

'You have been putting on some weight, haven't you?'

c. 頭がいたくなってきました。

Atama ga itaku natte kimashita.

'I am getting a headache.'

Sentence (3) indicates that a certain situation has *continued* up until now. (4) indicates that a certain change has begun to take place and has continued up until now.

Since *-te kuru* does indicate a "change" or a "process," what is the difference between *-te kuru* and *yoo ni naru*? Consider the following sentences.

(5) a. 分かってきました。

Wakatte kimashita.

'I am beginning to understand.'

b. 分かりました。

Wakarimashita.

'I understand. / I understood.'

c. 分かるようになりました。

Wakaru yoo ni narimashita.

'I came to understand.'

Sentence (5b) indicates an instantaneous event. Of the two forms which indicate process/change, (5c) implies that the change took place some time in the past and is essentially complete. Sentence (5a), on the other hand, relates the change to the immediate presence of the speaker "here and now."

(6) a. 寒くなりましたね。
   Samuku narimashita ne.
   'It has become cold, hasn't it?'
   b. 寒くなってきましたね。
   Samuku natte kimashita ne.
   'It has become cold, hasn't it?'

The speaker might utter either (6a) or (6b) when the weather turns chilly in the fall. Sentence (6a) presents the change as more or less a completed fact, while by uttering (6b), the speaker implies that the change is continuing to take place right here and now and that the speaker is in the middle of it. Sentence (6b) thus gives a sense that the change is a more immediate experience.

10. *TO* vs. *TOKI*

The English temporal expression "when" has several Japanese equivalents. Among them, *to* vs. *toki* proves to be particularly problematic for students of Japanese, as they are both acceptable in sentences such as (1) and (2).

(1) a. 家へ帰ると
   Uchi e kaeru to
   b. 家へ帰った時
   Uchi e kaetta toki
   母が御馳走を作ってくれました。
   haha ga gochisoo o tsukutte kuremashita.
   'When I returned home, my mother prepared a feast for me.'

(2) 太郎は家へ $\left\{\begin{array}{l}\text{a. 帰ると}\\ \text{b. 帰った時}\end{array}\right\}$ 電話をかけた。

$\textit{Taroo wa uchi e} \left\{\begin{array}{l}\text{a. } \textit{kaeru to}\\ \text{b. } \textit{kaetta toki}\end{array}\right\} \textit{denwa o kaketa.}$

'Taroo made a telephone call when he returned home.'

One of the biggest differences between *to* and *toki* is the temporal relationship between *to/toki* clauses and the main clause. In $[S_1$ *toki* $S_2]$, S_2 is simultaneous or prior to S_1 if S_1 is in the present tense, and S_2 follows S_1 if S_1 is in the past tense. In $[S_1$ *to* $S_2]$, S_2 always follows S_1 in temporal sequencing. Hence, the following.

(3) 説明する $\left\{\begin{array}{l}\text{時}\\ *\text{と}\end{array}\right\}$ たくさん例をあげます。

$\textit{Setsumei suru} \left\{\begin{array}{l}\textit{toki}\\ *\textit{to}\end{array}\right\} \textit{takusan rei o agemasu.}$

'I give lots of examples when I explain.'

(4) 日本では人の家へ遊びに $\left\{\begin{array}{l}\text{行く時}\\ *\text{行くと}\end{array}\right\}$ おみやげを持って行きます。

$\textit{Nihon de wa hito no uchi e asobi ni} \left\{\begin{array}{l}\textit{iku toki}\\ *\textit{iku to}\end{array}\right\}$

$\textit{omiyage o motte ikimasu.}$

'In Japan, we bring gifts when we visit people.'

In (3), you use examples while explaining. In (4), you bring a gift to someone's house—i.e., S_1 and S_2 occur simultaneously. Hence, *to* is not appropriate since the use of *to* would imply that S_2 (giving examples, bringing a gift) will occur after S_1 is completed.

Now, consider the following example.

(5) 田中さんが部屋に $\left\{\begin{array}{l}\text{a. 入って来ると}\\ \text{b. 入って来た時}\end{array}\right\}$ 急に静かになった。

$$Tanaka\text{-}san \ ga \ heya \ ni \left\{ \begin{array}{l} a \ . \quad haitte \ kuru \ to \\ b \ . \quad haitte \ kita \ toki \end{array} \right\} kyuu \ ni$$

shizuka ni natta.

'When Mr. Tanaka came in, the room became quiet suddenly.'

In (5), both *toki* and *to* are acceptable since S_2 follows S_1 in temporal sequence. In such cases, the use of *to* indicates that there is an *inevitable relationship* between S_1 and S_2, such as cause and effect, antecedent-consequence, etc. In (5), *to* implies that Tanaka's entering the room was the cause for the room becoming quiet. *Toki*, on the other hand, merely states "when, at which time" something happens (happened). Hence (5b) could be an answer to "when did the room become quiet ?" (5b) merely states that Tanaka's entering the room and the room becoming quiet happened at the same time : they could have been merely coincidental.

In the following, *to* is fine but not *toki*.

(6) その時のことを $\left\{ \begin{array}{l} 思い出すと \\ ^*思い出す時(は) \\ ^*思い出した時(は) \end{array} \right\}$ なつかしい。

$$Sono \quad toki \quad no \quad koto \quad o \left\{ \begin{array}{l} omoidasu \ to \\ ^* omoidasu \ toki \ (wa) \\ ^* omoidashita \ toki \ (wa) \end{array} \right\}$$

natsukashii.

'When I think back of that time, I feel nostalgic.'

What this sentence is trying to say is that there is an inevitable relationship between the two sentences—i.e., remembering about the time makes one feel nostalgic. The sentence is not concerned about *at which time* one gets nostalgic. Hence, *to* but not *toki* is appropriate.

Going back to examples (1) and (2), there are subtle differences between (a) and (b) sentences. (1a) indicates that "going home" and "mother preparing a feast" are somehow inevitably linked——i.e., this was a customary occurrence. (1b) merely states a time point when (his) mother prepared the feast. In (2a), Taroo's going home and his making a telephone call are presented as somehow related—— as a natural sequence of events, while (2b) answers the question of "when" he made a telephone call.

BIBLIOGRAPHY
Kunihiro (1982)

CONJUNCTIONS AND RELATED EXPRESSIONS

11. *NONI* vs. *KEREDO*

Both *noni* and *keredo* are conjunctions meaning *but* or *although*. *Noni*, however, imposes a strong sense of "contrary to expectation".

(1) 日本人なのに，漢字が書けない。
Nihonjin na noni, kanji ga kakenai.
'He is Japanese, but he cannot write kanji.'

Sentence (1) implies that there is a general expectation that if one is Japanese, one will be able to write kanji. (1) negates this expectation.

Because of this expectation, *noni* is highly evaluative, and expresses the speaker's various sentiments such as frustration, disappointment, surprise, etc. It often carries a negative sense that it should not be this way, it should be otherwise, that something is strange, or the like.

(2) a. 勉強したのにできなかった。
Benkyoo shita noni dekinakatta.
b. 勉強したけれどできなかった。
Benkyoo shita keredo dekinakatta.
'Although I studied, I could not do it well.'
(3) a. 寒いのに出かけた。
Samui noni dekaketa.
b. 寒いけれど出かけた。

Samui keredo dekaketa.
'Although it was cold, (he) went out.'

By uttering (2a), the speaker expresses his frustration/disappoint-
ment that he did not do better——that he should have done better
because he studied. (2b), on the other hand, simply states a fact.
Sentence (2b) simply describes what happened. (3a) implies that the
speaker hoped (he) would not go, but (he) did, so the speaker feels
sorry——wishes it would have been otherwise.

In many cases, therefore, *noni* and *keredo* are not interchangeable.

(4)　a．日本人なのに漢字が書けないんですか。
　　　　Nihonjin na noni kanji ga kakenai n desu ka ?
　　　b．*日本人だけれど漢字が書けないんですか。
　　　　**Nihonjin da keredo kanji ga kakenai n desu ka ?*
　　　　'He is Japanese and can't write kanji ?'

(5)　a．*ちょっと高いのに買いませんか。
　　　　**Chotto takai noni kaimasen ka ?*
　　　b．ちょっと高いけれど買いませんか。
　　　　Chotto takai keredo kaimasen ka ?
　　　　'It's a little expensive, but won't you buy it ?'

(6)　a．その庭は大きくなかったけれど池や木がありました。
　　　　*Sono niwa wa ookikunakatta keredo ike ya ki ga
　　　　　arimashita.*
　　　b．?*その庭は大きくなかったのに池や木がありました。
　　　　?**Sono niwa wa ookikunakatta noni ike ya ki ga
　　　　　arimashita.*
　　　　'It was not a large garden, but it had a pond and trees.'

(7)　a．このアパートはきれいだけれど便利じゃありません。
　　　　Kono apaato wa kirei da keredo benri ja arimasen.
　　　b．*このアパートはきれいなのに便利じゃありません。
　　　　**Kono apaato wa kirei na noni benri ja arimasen.*
　　　　'This apartment is pretty but it is not convenient.'

42

Sentence (4) expresses the speaker's surprise and hence a value judgment that any Japanese should be able to write kanji, and so *noni* but not *keredo* is appropriate.   In (5), the speaker cannot imply his value judgment since the main sentence is an invitation.   In cases where the main sentence is an invitation, question, request, *keredo* should be used.   Sentences (6) and (7) are objective descriptions of facts, and hence *keredo*, but not *noni*, is appropriate.

One should be especially careful in using *noni* in describing one's own actions.

(8) 私はきのうレストランへ行った。食べものはおいしかった けれど(*のに)一セントもチップをおかなかった。
    Watashi wa kinoo resutoran e itta.   Tabemono wa oishi-
    *katta keredo / * noni issento mo chippu o okanakatta.*
    'I went to a restaurant yesterday.   The food was good, but I did not leave any tip.'

(9) きのうはひどい雨だったけれど (*のに) 出かけた。
    *Kinoo wa hidoi ame datta keredo / * noni dekaketa.*
    'It rained hard yesterday, but *I* went out.'

Suppose (8) and (9) are entries in one's diary.   One is reporting about one's own actions, and, in such cases, the use of *noni* is unnatural. If *noni* is used here, it sounds as if the speaker/writer is blaming himself/herself or feeling a strong sense of remorse about what he/she did or did not do.   Unless one wants to convey such sentiment (disapproval, blame, shame, frustration or the like) about one's own actions, one should avoid using *noni* in reporting what one did (or did not do).

12. *NONI* vs. *KUSENI*

Both *noni* and *kuseni* express the idea of 'although', 'in spite of the fact that.'

(1) a. 日本人のくせに日本語が話せない。
         Nihonjin no kuseni nihongo ga hanasenai.
      b. 日本人なのに日本語が話せない。
         Nihonjin na noni nihongo ga hanasenai.
         'Although he is Japanese, he cannot speak Japanese.'

(2) a. 学生のくせにちっとも勉強しない。
         Gakusei no kuseni chittomo benkyoo shinai.
      b. 学生なのにちっとも勉強しない。
         Gakusei na noni chittomo benkyoo shinai.
         'Although he is a student, he does not study at all.'

In both cases, what you would expect from the first clause is negated in the second clause.

The function of *kuseni* is to express the speaker's feeling of contempt toward the subject of the sentence or to put someone down as someone who possesses an undesirable trait, abnormality, defective character or the like. Hence, *kuseni* focuses on the person himself (his inherent or acquired quality), while *noni* focuses not on the person but on the fact that an expected consequence does not hold, resulting in speaker sentiment such as surprise, disappointment, frustration, etc.

Consider the following sentences.

(3) a. *アメリカ人のくせに日本語が上手です。
         *Amerikajin no kuseni nihongo ga joozu desu.
      b. アメリカ人なのに日本語が上手です。
         Amerikajin na noni nihongo ga joozu desu.
         'Although (he) is an American, (he) speaks Japanese well.'

For someone to be able to speak Japanese will not lead one to consider that person as an undesirable American. Hence, *kuseni* is unacceptable here.

(4)   a. 知っているくせに教えてくれない。
        Shitte iru kuseni oshiete kurenai.
     b. 知っているのに教えてくれない。
        Shitte iru noni oshiete kurenai.
        'Although he knows, he will not tell me.'

(5)   a. 十年日本に住んでいたくせに日本語を一言も覚えなかった。
        Juunen nihon ni sunde ita kuseni nihongo o hitokoto mo oboenakatta.
     b. 十年日本に住んでいたのに日本語を一言も覚えなかった。
        Juunen nihon ni sunde ita noni nihongo o hito koto mo oboenakatta.
        'Although he lived in Japan for ten years, he did not learn a single word of Japanese.'

(4b) expresses the speaker's irritation or frustration at the fact that the person does not tell anything. (4a) expresses the speaker's feeling of contempt or anger toward the person, implying that he lacks a certain decency as a person. Similarly, (5a) is an outright criticism of the person. In (5b), on the other hand, the speaker's attention is simply on the unexpected consequence of not having learned a single word of Japanese, with the accompanying feeling of surprise or regret.

13. *NO KA* vs. *SEI KA* ─────────────────

Observe the following sentences.

(1) a. 体が弱いせいか，クラスをよく休む。

   Karada ga yowai sei ka, kurasu o yoku yasumu.

   '(He) is often absent from class, perhaps because he is sickly.'

   b. 体が弱いのか，クラスをよく休む。

   Karada ga yowai no ka, kurasu o yoku yasumu.

   '(He) is often absent from class, perhaps because he is sickly.'

(2) a. 試験が悪かったせいか，元気がない。

   Shiken ga warukatta sei ka, genki ga nai.

   b. 試験が悪かったのか，元気がない。

   Shiken ga warukatta no ka, genki ga nai.

   '(He) looks dispirited, perhaps because he did badly on the exam.'

In both (a) and (b) sentences above, the first clause is viewed as a possible reason or cause for the second clause.

There are two basic differences between these two constructions. First, *sei ka* implies that the result is negative, while *no ka* can be used with either a negative or a positive result.   Hence, (3a) is odd.

(3) a. *試験が良かったせいか，うれしそうだ。

   **Shiken ga yokatta sei ka, ureshi soo da.*

   b. 試験が良かったのか，うれしそうだ。

   Shiken ga yokatta no ka, ureshi soo da.

   '(He) looks happy, perhaps because he did well on the exam.'

Secondly, in $[S_1$ *sei ka* $S_2]$, the speaker knows that S_1 is true. What the speaker is not sure about is whether S_1 is the actual reason for S_2. In $[S_1$ *no ka* $S_2]$, on the other hand, the speaker does not know if S_1 is true——S_1 is only a conjecture on the part of the speaker. So, in (1a), the speaker knows for a fact that the person is sickly; he does not know, however, if that is a real reason for the person's absence. In (1b), the speaker does not know for sure if the person is indeed sickly——he simply assumes that that might be the case.

Hence, a fact cannot be introduced by *no ka*, while a non-fact cannot be introduced by *sei ka*.

(4)　a.　月曜日のせいか，学生はみんな元気がない。

　　　　Getsuyoobi no sei ka, gakusei wa minna genki ga nai.

　　b.　*月曜日なのか，学生はみんな元気がない。

　　　　*Getsuyoobi na no ka, gakusei wa minna genki ga nai.

　　　　'The students look tired, perhaps because it is Monday.'

It is often the case that students do not respond as well on Mondays (for some reason). So, the teacher can say (4a) on Mondays, but not (4b).

Similarly, the speaker's own actions are facts——they are not subject to his own conjectures. Hence *no ka* is not acceptable when the speaker is talking about his own actions, as in (5).

(5)　a.　(私は) きのうの晩徹夜したせいか頭がはっきりしない。

　　　　(Watashi wa) kinoo no ban tetsuya shita sei ka atama ga hakkiri shinai.

　　b.　*(私は) きのうの晩徹夜したのか頭がはっきりしない。

　　　　*(Watashi wa) kinoo no ban tetsuya shita no ka atama ga hakkiri shinai

'My head is not clear, perhaps because I was up all night last night.'

Of course, (5b) becomes fine if someone else's action is talked about, as in (6).

(6) a. (田中さんは)きのうの晩徹夜したせいか今日ねむそうだ。

      (*Tanaka-san wa*) *kinoo no ban tetsuya shita sei ka kyoo nemu soo da.*

   b. (田中さんは)きのうの晩徹夜したのか，今日ねむそうだ。

      (*Tanaka-san wa*) *kinoo no ban tetsuya shita no ka, kyoo nemu soo da.*

      '(Mr. Tanaka) looks sleepy today, perhaps because he was up all night last night.'

14. *TAME NI* vs. *YOO NI* ————————————————

Tame ni means 'in order to' and *yoo ni* means 'so that.' *Tame ni* states the purpose of an action, while *yoo ni* implies that a certain consequence will hold as the result of an action. Hence, in [X *tame ni* Y], X represents an action which can be controlled by the subject of Y (i. e., can be brought about by the will of the subject of Y.) In [X *yoo ni* Y], X represents a state or an event which is beyond one's control.

(1) 新しい車を買う { ために / *ようにに } お金をためています。

    Atarashii kuruma o kau { *tame ni* / * *yoo ni* } *okane o tamete* *imasu.*

'I am saving money in order to buy a new car.'

(2) 日本語を勉強する $\left\{ \begin{array}{c} ためで \\ *ように \end{array} \right\}$ 日本へ行きます。

Nihongo o benkyoo suru $\left\{ \begin{array}{c} tame\ ni \\ *yoo\ ni \end{array} \right\}$ *nihon e ikimasu.*

'I will go to Japan in order to study Japanese.'

(3) みんなに分かる $\left\{ \begin{array}{c} ように \\ *ために \end{array} \right\}$ 話した。

Minna ni wakaru $\left\{ \begin{array}{c} yoo\ ni \\ *tame\ ni \end{array} \right\}$ *hanashita.*

'I talked so that everybody will understand.'

(4) 忘れない $\left\{ \begin{array}{c} ように \\ *ために \end{array} \right\}$ ノートに書いておいた。

Wasurenai $\left\{ \begin{array}{c} yoo\ ni \\ *tame\ ni \end{array} \right\}$ *nooto ni kaite oita.*

'I wrote (it) down in the notebook so that I would not forget.'

In (1), the purpose of one's saving money is to buy a new car. In (2), studying Japanese is the objective the speaker has in mind in going to Japan. In (3), the speaker talked with the hope that others would understand. Whether others will understand or not is clearly not controllable by the speaker's will. In (4), the speaker wrote it down with the hope that he would not forget. Whether one forgets or not is something which simply happens to one and cannot be determined by one's will.

The use of *tame ni* vs. *yoo ni* depends greatly on the kind of verb which precedes these expressions. If the verb in X is an action verb (e. g., *yomu, taberu, iku,* etc.), *tame ni* is used. *Yoo ni* would be typically used if the verb in X is in potential form (*dekiru,* (*tabe*) *rareru,* (*yom*)*eru,* etc.), in negative form or a stative verb, such as *wakaru.*

(5) 朝早く起きられる $\left\{ \begin{array}{l} {}^{*}\text{ために} \\ \text{ように} \end{array} \right\}$ 早く寝ます。

Asa hayaku okirareru $\left\{ \begin{array}{l} {}^{*}tame\ ni \\ yoo\ ni \end{array} \right\}$ hayaku nemasu.

'I go to sleep early so that I can get up early.'

(6) 病気にならない $\left\{ \begin{array}{l} {}^{*}\text{ために} \\ \text{ように} \end{array} \right\}$ 毎日運動をしています。

Byooki ni naranai $\left\{ \begin{array}{l} {}^{*}tame\ ni \\ yoo\ ni \end{array} \right\}$ mainichi undoo o shite

imasu.

'I exercise every day so that I won't get sick.'

If the subjects of X and Y are different, moreover, *yoo ni* is the appropriate form since one cannot normally control someone else's action.

(7) 学生が勉強する $\left\{ \begin{array}{l} {}^{*}\text{ために} \\ \text{ように} \end{array} \right\}$ 先生は毎日宿題を出す。

Gakusei ga benkyoo suru $\left\{ \begin{array}{l} {}^{*}tame\ ni \\ yoo\ ni \end{array} \right\}$ sensei wa mai-

nichi shukudai o dasu.

'Teachers give homework everyday so that students will study.'

Examine additional examples.

(8) a. もっとよく見るために前のほうへ行った。

Motto yoku miru tame ni mae no hoo e itta.

'I moved to the front in order to take a closer look.'

b. もっとよく見えるように前のほうへ行った。

Motto yoku mieru yoo ni mae no hoo e itta.

'I moved to the front so that I could see better.'

(9) a. 日本語を習うために日本へ行く。

Nihongo o narau tame ni nihon e iku.

'I am going to Japan in order to learn Japanese.'

b. 日本語が上手になるように一生懸命勉強している。

Nihongo ga joozu ni naru yoo ni isshoo kenmei benkyoo shite iru.

'I am studying hard so that my Japanese will improve.'

(10) a. 電気をつけるために家の中に入った。

Denki o tsukeru tame ni ie no naka ni haitta.

'I went into the house in order to turn the light on.'

b. 自然に電気がつくようにタイマーをかけた。

Shizen ni denki ga tsuku yoo ni taimaa o kaketa.

'I set the timer on so that the light will come on automatically.'

Note that, in Japanese, improving one's language ability is a state which happens to one and is not a state one can bring about by one's will. Hence, *yoo ni* but not *tame ni* should be used in (9b).

BIBLIOGRAPHY

Kunihiro *et al.* (1982)

15. *TAME NI, NO NI* vs. *NI WA* ───────────

Both *tame ni* and *no ni* are frequently used to state a purpose or goal of a certain action.

(1) a. 日本人は御飯を食べるためにおはしを使います。

Nihonjin wa gohan o taberu tame ni ohashi o tsukaimasu.

'Japanese use chopsticks for the purpose of eating.'

b. 日本人は御飯を食べるのにおはしを使います。

Nihonjin wa gohan o taberu no ni ohashi o tsukaimasu.

'Japanese use chopsticks to eat.'

While *tame ni* states a clear *objective* one has in mind in doing
something, *no ni* simply states an end to which an action is directed.
Hence, a sentence with *tame ni* might answer a question of "why" a
certain action is being taken, while a sentence with *no ni* might
answer a question of "how" one does things——standard procedure
one employs, how long/much it takes to achieve a certain goal, or
the like. So, in (1a), we know that Japanese use chopsticks but
why?——for the purpose of eating. In (1b), we know people eat by
various means. How do Japanese do it?——by chopsticks.

Following are some more examples.

(2) その病気をなおす $\left\{ \begin{array}{c} ためtrueに \\ {}_?のに \end{array} \right\}$ いろいろなことをやってみ
ました。

Sono byooki o naosu $\left\{ \begin{array}{c} tame\ ni \\ {}_?\ no\ ni \end{array} \right\}$ iroirona koto o yatte
mimashita.

'I tried various things in order to treat that illness.'

(3) 東京へ行く $\left\{ \begin{array}{c} {}^*ためtrueに \\ のに \end{array} \right\}$ 二時間もかかりました。

Tookyoo e iku $\left\{ \begin{array}{c} {}^*tame\ ni \\ no\ ni \end{array} \right\}$ nijikan mo kakarimashita.

'It took as many as two hours to go to Tokyo.'

(4) 駅へ行く $\left\{ \begin{array}{c} {}^{??}ために \\ のに \end{array} \right\}$ バスに乗りました。

Eki e iku $\left\{ \begin{array}{c} {}^{??}tame\ ni \\ no\ ni \end{array} \right\}$ basu ni norimashita.

'I took the bus to go to the station.'

Sentence (2) states a specific purpose for the speaker's having tried
various things, and so *tame ni* is appropriate. In (3) and (4), the

question is not why it takes two hours or why one takes the bus. Rather, it asks *how* one gets to Tokyo or *how* one gets to the station.

Now, when the main predicate is an adjectival predicate such as *ii* 'good', *benri da* 'is convenient', *tekitoo da* 'is appropriate', etc., *no ni* is preferred. These sentences express a certain evaluation of a place, a person, or the like.

(5)　ここは子供を育てる $\left\{ \begin{matrix} のに \\ *ために \end{matrix} \right\}$ いい。

　　　Koko wa kodomo o sodateru $\left\{ \begin{matrix} no\ ni \\ *tame\ ni \end{matrix} \right\}$ *ii.*

　　　'This is a good place for raising children.'

(6)　キャンパスに近いアパートは歩いて通う $\left\{ \begin{matrix} のに \\ *ために \end{matrix} \right\}$ 便利 だ。

　　　Kyanpasu ni chikai apaato wa aruite kayou $\left\{ \begin{matrix} no\ ni \\ *tame\ ni \end{matrix} \right\}$ *benri da.*

　　　'Apartments which are close to campus are convenient for walking to school.'

The expression *ni wa* is similar to *no ni*, but expresses a contrast or a topic.

(7)　マジソンは子供を育てる $\left\{ \begin{matrix} a.\ のに \\ b.\ には \end{matrix} \right\}$ いいところだ。

　　　Majison wa kodomo o sodateru $\left\{ \begin{matrix} a.\ no\ ni \\ b.\ ni\ wa \end{matrix} \right\}$ *ii tokoro da.*

　　　'Madison is a good place to raise children.'

(8)　子供を育てる $\left\{ \begin{matrix} a.\ には \\ b.\ {}^?のに \end{matrix} \right\}$ マジソンがいい。

$$Kodomo\ o\ sodateru \begin{Bmatrix} \text{a}. & ni\ wa \\ \text{b}. & ^?no\ ni \end{Bmatrix} Majison\ ga\ ii.$$

'If we are talking about raising children, Madison is good.'

Wa in *ni wa* in (7b) is contrastive. (7b) has the implication that Madison is a good place for raising children but perhaps not for other things. In (8a), on the other hand, *wa* is thematic. (8a) says that as for raising children, Madison is a good place.

16. -*TE* vs. -*TA* (*GA*)

Two or more sentences can be conjoined by using -*te* forms as in (1).

(1) 太郎が買いものをして，花子が料理をした。
Taroo ga kaimono o shite, Hanako ga ryoori o shita.
'Taroo did the shopping and Hanako did the cooking.'

The function of the -*te* form is to link two or more sentences. When sentences are conjoined by the -*te* form, there has to be some meaningful relationship between the sentences. If no meaningful connection can be assigned to them, the sentence sounds odd, as in (2).

(2) *太郎が買いものをして，花子が試験におちた。
**Taroo ga kaimono o shite, Hanako ga shiken ni ochita.*
'Taroo did the shopping and Hanako flunked the exam.'

Sentence (2) would only make sense in a universe where shopping and taking an exam are somehow related.

Some of the meaningful relationships which hold between two sentences conjoined by the -*te* form are:

a) Cause-effect (the first clause is the reason/cause for the second clause.)

(3) おなかが痛くて，歩けない。

    Onaka ga itakute, arukenai.

    'I have a stomachache and can't walk.'

(4) 病気で学校を休んだ。

    Byooki de gakkoo o yasunda.

    'I was sick and was absent from school.'

b) Sequence (the first clause happens first, and then the second clause happens.)

(5) 図書館へ行って，勉強した。

    Toshokan e itte, benkyoo shita.

    'I went to the library and studied.'

(6) 家へ帰って，宿題をした。

    Uchi e kaette, shukudai o shita.

    'I went home and did my homework.'

c) Statements about a common topic.

(7) このレストランは安くておいしい。

    Kono resutoran wa yasukute oishii.

    'This restaurant is cheap and good.'

(8) 私がピアノをひいて，メリーが歌をうたった。

    Watashi ga piano o hiite, Merii ga uta o utatta.

    'I played the piano and Mary sang a song.'

(9) 先生が聞いて，学生が答える。

    Sensei ga kiite, gakusei ga kotaeru.

    'The teacher askes questions and the students answer.'

In (7), being cheap and being delicious are two statements about the same topic (restaurant) of the sentence.   In (8) and (9), the common topic is not overtly spelled out.   The common topic in (8) is the "performance" and "classroom procedure" in (9).

Hence, students should be careful not to conjoin every and any sentence with *-te*, although children often tend to do so. Consider the following sentences.

(10) a. きのうは午後映画へ行った。

    Kinoo wa gogo eiga e itta.

    'Yesterday we went to a movie in the afternoon.'

  b. レストランで食事をして，そのあとパーティーへ行って，いろいろおもしろい話をした。

    Resutoran de shokuji o shite, sono ato paatii e itte, iroiro omoshiroi hanashi o shita.

    'We had dinner in a restaurant, and then we went to a party and talked about many interesting things.'

  c. 九時半に $\left\{\begin{array}{l} ^{??}帰って, \\ 帰ったが, \end{array}\right\}$ とてもいい日だった。

    Kuji-han ni $\left\{\begin{array}{l} ^{??}kaette, \\ kaetta\ ga, \end{array}\right\}$ *totemo ii hi datta.*

    'We went home at 9:30 p. m., and it was a very interesting day.'

In (10c), since the second clause describes a certain emotional feeling, the *-te* form tends to be interpreted as "causal." However, "returning home at nine o'clock" is not the cause for "feeling good about the day." Hence, the *-te* form is not appropriate here.

(11) 「何か言葉を間違ったかな」と友人に $\left\{\begin{array}{l} a.\ \ 聞いたところ \\ b.\ ^{??}聞いて \end{array}\right\}$ 友人は，「いや大丈夫だったよ」と言った。

    "Nanika kotoba o machigatta ka na" to yuujin ni $\left\{\begin{array}{l} a.\ \ kiita\ tokoro \\ b.\ ^{??}kiite \end{array}\right\}$ *yuujin wa 'iya daijoobu datta yo" to itta.*

'I asked my friend, "Did I make any mistakes ?", and my friend answered "No, you did fine." '

The only possible interpretation for (11) is that both clauses are statements about a common topic. (11), however, is not a description of a common topic, such as the procedure for doing something. Rather, in (11), the second clause is the main point and the first clause provides background for the second clause. In such cases, *te* is not appropriate.

17. *TEMO* vs. *KEREDO*

Adjective/verb-*temo* is sometimes used to conjoin two contrasting sentences.

(1)   a . アメリカへ行ってきても英語はあまり上手にならない でしょう。

Amerika e itte kitemo eigo wa amari joozu ni naranai deshoo.

'Even if you go to America, your English will not improve much.'

       b . アメリカへ行ってきても，英語はあまり上手にならな かった。

Amerika e itte kitemo, eigo wa amari joozu ni naranakatta.

'Even though (I) went to America, my English did not improve much.'

While (1a) talks of a hypothetical event, (1b) refers to a specific event which has already happened—i.e., someone has gone to America and come back. In the latter case, the sentence (1b) can be paraphrased using *keredo* or *noni*.

(2) アメリカへ行ってきた けれど/のに 英語はあまり上手に
　　ならなかった。

Amerika e itte kita keredo/noni eigo wa amari joozu ni naranakatta.

'Although (he) went to America, (his) English did not improve much.'

Temo and *keredo/noni*, however, are not interchangeable in all non-hypothetical cases. In the following, *temo* is unacceptable.

(3) ビールを $\left\{ \begin{array}{l} 飲まないけれど \\ {}^*飲まなくても \end{array} \right\}$ バーへ行った。

Biiru o $\left\{ \begin{array}{l} nomanai\ keredo \\ {}^*nomanakutemo \end{array} \right\}$ *baa e itta.*

'Even though I don't drink beer, I went to a bar.'

(4) 大きく $\left\{ \begin{array}{l} ないけれど, \\ {}^*なくても, \end{array} \right\}$ とてもきれいな町です。

Ookiku $\left\{ \begin{array}{l} nai\ keredo, \\ {}^*nakutemo, \end{array} \right\}$ *totemo kirei na machi desu.*

'Although it is not big, it is a pretty town.'

Now, contrast sentences with *temo* and those with *keredo/noni*.

(5) いろいろ説明 $\left\{ \begin{array}{ll} a. & しても \\ b. & したのに \end{array} \right\}$ 分かってくれなかった。

Iroiro setsumei $\left\{ \begin{array}{ll} a. & shitemo \\ b. & shita\ noni \end{array} \right\}$ *wakatte kurenakatta.*

'Although I explained in various ways, (he) did not understand.'

(6) 手紙を $\left\{ \begin{array}{ll} a. & 出しても \\ b. & 出したけれど \end{array} \right\}$ 返事が来ない。

$$Tegami \ o \begin{Bmatrix} a. & dashitemo \\ b. & dashita \ keredo \end{Bmatrix} henji \ ga \ konai.$$

'Even though I sent (him) a letter, there has not been any reply.'

(7) 会ったことが $\begin{Bmatrix} a. & なくても \\ b. & なかったけれど \end{Bmatrix}$ 嫁に行かなければならなかった。

$$Atta \ koto \ ga \begin{Bmatrix} a. & nakutemo \\ b. & nakatta \ keredo \end{Bmatrix} yome \ ni \ ikanakereba \ naranakatta.$$

'Although I had not met him, I had to marry him.'

While *keredo/noni* introduces facts as such, *temo* has a sense of "no matter how ...", "whether ... or not ...," "be that as it may ...," or the like. (5b), for example, states two facts—that the speaker explained and that the hearer did not understand. (5a), on the other hand, gives the sense that no matter how hard (he) tried, (he) could not make the hearer understand. (7b) simply contrasts two facts. In (7a), she had to get married whether she had met him or not—no matter what the circumstances were.

Now, in sentences (3) and (4), the objective of the speaker is simply to convey two contrasting facts. Hence, *temo* is unacceptable in (3) and (4).

PARTICLES

18. *DE DAKE* vs. *DAKE DE*

A particle can be positioned either before or after *dake*, as in (1) and (2).

(1) バスでだけ行けます。
 Basu de dake ikemasu.
 'You can get there only by bus.'

(2) バスだけで行けます。
 Basu dake de ikemasu.
 'You can get there by bus alone.'

There are subtle differences between such sentences. When a particle precedes *dake*, it means 'only.' When a particle follows *dake*, it means 'alone, just.' So, sentence (1) means that the only way to get to this place is by bus——no other means of transportation is possible. Sentence (2) means that there are other methods of transportation but one can go there by bus alone; one does not have to take a train, for example. (Kuno & Monane 1979 : 119.)

Following are some more examples.

(3) a. 受験勉強は学校でだけできます。
 Jukenbenkyoo wa gakkoo de dake dekimasu.
 'The only place you can prepare for an entrance examination is at school——you cannot do it at any other place.'

 b. 受験勉強は学校だけでできます。

Jukenbenkyoo wa gakkoo dake de dekimasu.

'You can prepare for an entrance examination at various places but doing it at school alone is sufficient.'

So, in order to express the idea that something is not sufficient to attain a desired goal, *dake* + Particle should be used.

(4)　ナイフだけでは食べられない。

Naifu dake de wa taberarenai.

'You can't eat with a knife alone (you need a fork also.)'

(5)　サラダだけではおなかが一杯になりません。

Sarada dake de wa onaka ga ippai ni narimasen.

'Salad is not enough to fill me up.'

Particle + *dake*, moreover, is not generally used in past-tense form since it describes a general truth.

(6)　a.　バスだけで行きました。

　　　　Basu dake de ikimashita.

　　　　'I went by bus alone.'

　　b.　*バスでだけ行きました。

　　　　**Basu de dake ikimashita.*

This semantic difference is significantly weakened when *dake* occurs with other particles such as *to*, *ni*, *kara*, etc. There is not much difference between (7a) and (7b), for example.

(7)　a.　母にだけ話します。

　　　　Haha ni dake hanashimasu.

　　b.　母だけに話します。

　　　　Haha dake ni hanashimasu.

　　　　'I will tell (it) only to (my) mother.'

In some contexts, however, the difference is preserved.

(8)　医者にだけはなりたくない。

Isha ni dake wa naritakunai.

'The only thing I don't want to be is a doctor.'

(9) 医者だけにはなりたくない。

Isha dake ni wa naritakunai.

'The only thing I don't want to be is a doctor./I don't want to be just a doctor.'

Sentence (8) means that (I) don't mind becoming anything but a doctor; doctor is one profession (I) don't want to take up. Sentence (9) can mean that (I) want to become a doctor as well as something else.

> **BIBLIOGRAPHY**
> Kuno & Monane (1979)

19. *NI* vs. *DE*

The location of an action is marked by *de* while the location of existence is marked by *ni*.

(1) a. レストランで食べました。

Resutoran de tabemashita.

'I ate at a restaurant.'

b. レストランにいます。

Resutoran ni imasu.

'(I) am in a restaurant.'

Some verbs characteristically take *ni*, as in the following examples.

(2) アメリカに住んでいます。

Amerika ni sunde imasu.

'(We) live in America.'

(3) いすにかけて下さい。

Isu ni kakete kudasai.

'Please sit on a chair.'

(4) 駅の前に立っています。

Eki no mae ni tatte imasu.

'(He) is standing in front of the station.'

Some verbs occur with either *ni* or *de*, but with clear differences in meaning.

(5) a. 家にあります。

Uchi ni arimasu.

'(It) is at (my) house.'

    b. 家であります。

Uchi de arimasu.

'(It) will be held at (my) house.'

(5a) says that something exists in the house while (5b) says that some event (e.g., party) will be held.

(6) a. 田中さんの家に赤ちゃんが生まれた。

Tanaka-san no uchi ni akachan ga umareta.

'A baby was born to the Tanaka family.'

    b. 田中さんの家で赤ちゃんが生まれた。

Tanaka-san no uchi de akachan ga umareta.

'The birth took place at Tanaka's house.'

(7) a. 机の上に書いた。

Tsukue no ue ni kaita.

'(I) wrote it onto the desk.'

    b. 机の上で書いた。

Tsukue no ue de kaita.

'(I) wrote it on the desk.'

(8) a. 部屋にたなを作った。

Heya ni tana o tsukutta.

'(I) made shelves for the room.'

b. 部屋でたなを作った。

Heya de tana o tsukutta.

'(I) made shelves in the room.'

(6a)-(8a), with *ni*, indicate that the result of an action belongs (exists) to the locative noun. *De*, on the other hand, simply indicates that an action took place at that place. In (6a), then, the baby is Tanaka's, while (6b) simply indicates that an event of childbirth took place at Tanaka's house——the baby could be somebody else's. (7a) indicates that the writing was done directly onto the desk, while (7b) indicates that an action of writing something down on paper took place on top of the desk.

20. *NI (hanasu)* vs. *TO (hanasu)*

The particle *ni*, as is exemplified in example (1), indicates a goal or an end point.

(1) a. 花子は太郎に本をあげた。

　　　Hanako wa Taroo ni hon o ageta.

　　　'Hanako gave a book to Taroo.'

　　b. 花子は太郎に本を見せた。

　　　Hanako wa Taroo ni hon o miseta.

　　　'Hanako showed a book to Taroo.'

　　c. 花子は太郎に勝った。

　　　Hanako wa Taroo ni katta.

　　　'Hanako won over Taroo.'

In (1), the action is directed toward Taroo, but no action takes place from Taroo's side. Hence, in (1), the action is *unidirectional*.

Some verbs, on the other hand, mark an NP with *to*, as in (2).

(2)　a．花子は太郎と結婚した。

　　　　Hanako wa Taroo to kekkon shita.

　　　　'Hanako married Taroo.'

　　　b．花子は太郎と喧嘩した。

　　　　Hanako wa Taroo to kenkashita.

　　　　'Hanako quarreled with Taroo.'

　　　c．花子は太郎と話し合った。

　　　　Hanako wa Taroo to hanashiatta.

　　　　'Hanako talked things over with Taroo.'

Here, *to* indicates that Taroo is as equal a participant in the action as Hanako. An action is initiated from both Hanako and Taroo. In (2a), if Hanako married Taroo, it must be true that Taroo married Hanako. In other words, the action is *reciprocal*.

This difference is reflected in cases where both *ni* and *to* are possible as in (3)-(5).

(3)　a．花子は太郎に会った。

　　　　Hanako wa Taroo ni atta.

　　　　'Hanako met Taroo.'

　　　b．花子は太郎と会った。

　　　　Hanako wa Taroo to atta.

　　　　'Hanako met Taroo.'

(4)　a．花子は太郎に話した。

　　　　Hanako wa Taroo ni hanashita.

　　　　'Hanako told Taroo.'

　　　b．花子は太郎と話した。

　　　　Hanako wa Taroo to hanashita.

　　　　'Hanako talked with Taroo.'

(5)　a．花子は太郎に恋愛している。

　　　　Hanako wa Taroo ni ren'ai shite iru.

　　　　'Hanako is in love with Taroo.'

　　　b．花子は太郎と恋愛している。

Hanako wa Taroo to ren'ai shite iru.
'Hanako and Taroo are mutually in love with each other.'

Ni is "unidirectional." So, (3a) implies that Taroo was at some place and Hanako went to see Taroo or ran into him. (3b) implies that Hanako and Taroo both came to meet at a common meeting place. (4a) is unidirectional, and says that Hanako told (it) to Taroo. Here Taroo is a passive participant. In (4b), both Hanako and Taroo were equally involved in talking. (5a) represents a case of Hanako's one-sided love, while (5b) represents a mutual affection between Hanako and Taroo. (Kuno 1973 : 103-104.)

A similar distinction can be observed in the following cases.

(6)　a．花子はお母さんに似ている。
　　　　　Hanako wa okaasan ni nite iru.
　　　　　'Hanako resembles her mother.'
　　　b．^{??}花子はお母さんと似ている。
　　　　　^{??}*Hanako wa okaasan to nite iru.*
　　　　　'Hanako resembles her mother.'
(7)　a．日本はアメリカに比べると…。
　　　　　Nihon wa amerika ni kuraberu to, ...
　　　b．日本はアメリカと比べると…。
　　　　　Nihon wa amerika to kuraberu to, ...
　　　　　'If we compare Japan with America, ...'

Ni indicates that NP-*ni* is the basis by which something is compared. Hence *ni* has a psychological priority. *To* indicates that both NPs are on equal basis. So, (6b) is strange with *to*, since, in general, one's mother would be a measuring stick by which one can be compared.

BIBLIOGRAPHY
Kuno (1973)

21. *-NI -O* vs. *-NO -O* (V-*te ageru*)

The verbs of giving *ageru* (or *yaru*) and *kureru* mark the indirect object (i.e., the recipient of a favor) by the particle *ni*, as in (1).

(1)　a．道子に英語を教えてあげた。

　　　Michiko ni eigo o oshiete ageta.

　　　'I taught Michiko English.'

　　b．弟に本を貸してやった。

　　　Otooto ni hon o kashite yatta.

　　　'I lent my brother a book.'

　　c．弟は(私に)セーターを買ってくれた。

　　　Otooto wa (watashi ni) seetaa o katte kureta.

　　　'My brother bought me a sweater.'

The indirect object NP, however, cannot always be marked by *ni*, as shown in the following examples.

(2)　a．道子 $\left\{ \begin{array}{c} *に \\ の \end{array} \right\}$ 部屋を掃除してあげた。

　　　Michiko $\left\{ \begin{array}{c} *ni \\ no \end{array} \right\}$ *heya o sooji shite ageta.*

　　　'I cleaned Michiko's room.'

　　b．弟 $\left\{ \begin{array}{c} *に \\ の \end{array} \right\}$ ペーパーをタイプしてやった。

　　　Otooto $\left\{ \begin{array}{c} *ni \\ no \end{array} \right\}$ *peepaa o taipu shite yatta.*

　　　'I typed my brother's paper.'

　　c．先生 $\left\{ \begin{array}{c} *に \\ の \end{array} \right\}$ 仕事を手伝ってさしあげた。

　　　Sensei $\left\{ \begin{array}{c} *ni \\ no \end{array} \right\}$ *shigoto o tetsudatte sashiageta.*

'I helped my teacher with his work.'

d. 姉は（私 $\left\{ \begin{array}{c} ^*に \\ の \end{array} \right\}$ ）勉強を見てくれた。

Ane wa (watashi $\left\{ \begin{array}{c} ^*ni \\ no \end{array} \right\}$) benkyoo o mite kure-

ta.

'My sister helped me with my study.'

In (2), the direct object (such as *heya*, *peepaa*, etc.) somehow *belongs* to the person (e.g., Michiko, otooto, etc.) In (2a), for example, the room belongs to Michiko, and the speaker did a favor for Michiko by cleaning her room.   In such cases, *ni* is inappropriate ; *no* should be used.

22. NO vs. (Prt)+NO

The following phrase is ambiguous in many ways.

(1) 先生の手紙

   sensei no tegami

It could be the letter written by the teacher or the letter written to the teacher.   To make the meaning clear, the particle has to be inserted before *no*, as in (2).

(2) a. 先生への手紙

     sensei e no tegami

     'the letter to the teacher'

   b. 先生からの手紙

     sensei kara no tegami

     'the letter from the teacher'

In many cases, expressions with or without the particle mean quite different things.　Examine the following examples.

(3)　a.　日本の切符を下さい。

　　　　Nihon no kippu o kudasai.

　　　　'Please give me a Japanese ticket.'

　　b.　日本までの切符を下さい。

　　　　Nihon made no kippu o kudasai.

　　　　'Please give me a ticket to Japan.'

(4)　a.　大統領の話はおもしろかった。

　　　　Daitooryoo no hanashi wa omoshirokatta.

　　　　'The President's talk was interesting.'

　　b.　大統領との話はおもしろかった。

　　　　Daitooryoo to no hanashi wa omoshirokatta.

　　　　'My talk with the President was interesting.'

(5)　a.　天気のためニューヨークへの飛行機は全部キャンセルされた。

　　　　Tenki no tame Nyuu Yooku e no hikooki wa zenbu kyanseru sareta.

　　　　'Because of the weather, all flights to New York were canceled.'

　　b.　天気のためニューヨークの飛行機は全部キャンセルされた。

　　　　Tenki no tame Nyuu Yooku no hikooki wa zenbu kyanseru sareta.

　　　　'Because of the weather, all flights in New York were canceled.'

23. *O -SASERU* vs. *NI -SASERU* ─────────

There are two types of causative sentences when the verb is an intransitive verb.

(1)　a．太郎は花子を買いものに行かせた。
　　　Taroo wa Hanako o kaimono ni ikaseta.
　　b．太郎は花子に買いものに行かせた。
　　　Taroo wa Hanako ni kaimono ni ikaseta.
　　　'Taroo made Hanako go shopping.'

(2)　a．太郎は花子を泣かせた。
　　　Taroo wa Hanako o nakaseta.
　　b．太郎は花子に泣かせた。
　　　Taroo wa Hanako ni nakaseta.
　　　'Taroo made Hanako cry.'

In (1a) and (2a), the causee is marked by the particle *o*, and they are called "*o*-causative" sentences. In (1b) and (2b), the causee is marked by *ni*, and hence they are called "*ni*-causative" sentences.

The most obvious implication of "*o*-causative" sentences is that a causee was "forced" or "coerced" to do something. So, in a situation where Hanako was *made* to go shopping against her will, (1a) will be an appropriate utterance. (2a) implies that Taroo did something physically or verbally, which *made* Hanako cry. "*Ni*-causative" sentences, on the other hand, imply that a causee acted, to some extent, on his/her own volition. So, (1b) implies that Hanako wanted to go shopping and Taroo simply "*let*" her go. (2b) implies that Hanako was willing to cry and Taroo "*let*" Hanako cry. (2b), therefore, would be strange unless Taroo is a play-director and Hanako, an actress.

"*O*-causative" sentences, however, do not always give a "coercive" sense. This can be shown by the following sentences.

(3) 太郎は何も言わないで花子を買いものに行かせた。

Taroo wa nani mo iwanaide Hanako o kaimono ni ikaseta.

'Taroo made Hanako go shopping without saying anything.'

(4) 先生は学生を席につかせた。

Sensei wa gakusei o seki ni tsukaseta.

'The teacher had the students sit down.'

In (3), Taroo is in a position to prevent Hanako from going shopping, but did not do anything to prevent it from happening——Taroo let it happen. In (4), the teacher is in a position to enforce some action without any coercion because of his/her inherent authority over the students. In both (3) and (4), no coercion is involved.

"*O*-causative" sentences, moreover, are sometimes used as "transitive" counterparts for intransitive verbs.

(5) 私は朝犬を歩かせます。

Watashi wa asa inu o arukasemasu.

'I walk my dog in the morning.'

(6) 子供を遊ばせるのは疲れます。

Kodomo o asobaseru no wa tsukaremasu.

'To let children play is tiring.'

In (5), there is no transitive verb such as "to walk a dog," and hence a causative construction is used to express this idea.

In most cases, the negation of "*o*-causative" sentences means that the causer did something by force to prevent an action from happening.

(7) 太郎は花子をパーティーへ行かせなかった。

Taroo wa Hanako o paatii e ikasenakatta.

'Taroo did not let Hanako go to a party.'

In (7), Taroo verbally or physically prevented Hanako from going to the party.

BIBLIOGRAPHY
Miyagawa (1984), Shibatani (1976)

24. O V-*tai* vs. GA V-*tai*

When *tai* is combined with a verb, an object of the verb can be marked either by *ga* or by *o*, as in (1).

(1)　a.　絵がかきたい。

　　　　E ga kakitai.

　　b.　絵をかきたい。

　　　　E o kakitai.

　　　　'I want to paint a picture.'

Compare (2) and (3).

(2)　a.　水が飲みたい。

　　　　Mizu ga nomitai.

　　　　'I want to drink water.'

　　b.　本が読みたい。

　　　　Hon ga yomitai.

　　　　'I want to read a book.'

　　c.　車が買いたい。

　　　　Kuruma ga kaitai.

　　　　'I want to buy a car.'

(3)　a.　電気を消したい。

　　　　Denki o keshitai.

　　　　'I want to turn the light off.'

　　b.　会社をやめたい。

Kaisha o yametai.
'I want to quit my job.'

c. 部屋を掃除したい。
   Heya o sooji shitai.
   'I want to clean my room.'

In (2), *ga* is preferred, while, in (3), *o* sounds better. This is because *ga* tends to be used when we express a basic desire, inner desire to satisfy our psychological and physical needs. In (3), however, we are not talking about our basic human desire. Rather, in (3), a specific object exists (e.g., a company) and the emphasis is on what you want to do with this specific object. When *o* is used, then, a verb/an action is emphasized. Consequently, when an action or a desire can be controlled by the speaker, as in (4), *o* should be used.

(4) a. 試験の前に宿題 を/*が してしまいたい。
       *Shiken no mae ni shukudai o / *ga shite shimaitai.*
       'I want to finish my homework before the exam.'

    b. お客さんが来る前におかし を /*が 買っておきたい。
       *Okyakusan ga kuru mae ni okashi o / *ga katte okitai.*
       'I want to buy some refreshments before the guests arrive.'

The difference between "spontaneous" vs. "controlled" can also be observed with potential constructions which also mark a direct object either with *ga* or *o*.

(5) a. 毎日やっているうちに自然に字 が /*を 書けるよう になった。
       *Mainichi yatte iru uchi ni shizen ni ji ga / *o kakeru yoo ni natta.*
       'As I practiced everyday, I became able to write characters gradually.'

b. 三年生が終わるまでに当用漢字 を / ?? *が 書けるよ
うにします。

*Sannensei ga owaru made ni tooyoo kanji o / ?? *ga*
kakeru yoo ni shimasu.

'I will try to learn Tooyoo kanji before I finish the third
year.'

(5a) represents a spontaneous result——he just happened to become
able to write. Here, *ga* is used. In (5b), the speaker has control
over his action of trying to learn Tooyoo kanji. Here, *o* is used.

BIBLIOGRAPHY
Makino (1975-76), Morita (1984)

25. *SAE, DEMO* vs. *MADE* ─────────

Noun + *sae/demo/made* all express the sense of 'even' in English.
So,

(1) 自分の名前さえ書けません。
Jibun no namae sae kakemasen.
'(He) can't even write his own name.'
(2) 子供でも知っています。
Kodomo demo shitte imasu.
'Even children know (it).'
(3) あの人の家にはプールまであります。
Ano hito no uchi ni wa puuru made arimasu.
'His house even has a swimming pool.'

There are, however, some differences.

First, *made* indicates an extent to which something is done, and means 'including—', 'up to the limit of —' or the like, and hence tends to designate an upper limit. So, sentence (3) means that his house has everything including a swimming pool.

Sae, on the other hand, indicates that an item focused by *sae* is what is *least expected* that a certain proposition holds. So, in (1), one's name is what you would least expect that someone cannot write —i.e., you normally expect peopole to be able to write his/her own name. Sentence (1) negates this expectation, and says that he can't write even his own name.

Now, *demo* has the connotation of "even if it were." So, in (2), even if it were a child, he would know (it). It strongly implies that *anybody* would know it. Because of this implication of "if", *demo* is not used to refer to a specific event, such as a past action.

(6)　＊田中さんでも来た。
　　　＊*Tanaka-san demo kita.*
　　　'Even Mr. Tanaka came.'

Compare the following sentences.

(7)　　a．百万円まで出すつもりだ。
　　　　　Hyaku man en made dasu tsumori da.
　　　　　'I intend to give up to a million yen.'
　　　　b．百万円でも出すつもりだ。
　　　　　Hyaku man en demo dasu tsumori da.
　　　　　'I intend to give even a million yen (perhaps more).'

In (7a), *made* defines an upper limit. The speaker is willing to give any amount up to one million yen. In (7b), the speaker is willing to give even if the amount is one million yen—he might be willing to give more.

(8)　　a．太郎まで来た。
　　　　　Taroo made kita.

'Everybody including Taroo came.'

b. *太郎でも来た。

  *Taroo demo kita.

  'Even Taroo came.'

c. 太郎さえ来た。

  Taroo sae kita.

  'Taroo, who is least expected to come, came.'

Sentence (8b) is unacceptable since *demo* does not occur with a past action.

(9)   a. *寝る暇までありません。

     *Neru hima made arimasen.

    b. *寝る暇でもありません。

     *Neru hima demo arimasen.

    c. 寝る暇さえありません。

     Neru hima sae arimasen.

     'I don't even have time to sleep.'

The whole point of (9) is not to enumerate what he does not have, but to indicate, for example, how busy he is because he does not have time to sleep, which everybody is expected to have. Hence, *sae* should be used in (9).

Finally, there is a version *de sae*, which is interchangeable with *sae*. *De sae*, however, is wider in usage than *sae*, and can be used even when *sae* by itself is unacceptable.

(10)   *子供さえ知っています。

   *Kodomo sae shitte imasu.

   子供でさえ知っています。

   Kodomo de sae shitte imasu.

   'Even children know it.'

26. *SHIKA* vs. *DAKE*

Shika means 'only' and *dake* means 'just' or 'only'. *Shika* requires the presence of a negative morpheme, while *dake* occurs both in negative and affirmative sentences. Sentences (1) and (2) illustrate this point.

(1) 田中さんしか $\left\{ \begin{array}{l} 来なかった。 \\ *来た。 \end{array} \right\}$

   Tanaka-san shika $\left\{ \begin{array}{l} ko-na-kat-ta. \\ *ki-ta. \end{array} \right\}$

   'Only Mr. Tanaka came.'

(2) 田中さんだけ $\left\{ \begin{array}{l} 来なかった。 \\ 来た。 \end{array} \right\}$

   Tanaka-san dake $\left\{ \begin{array}{l} ko-na-kat-ta. \\ ki-ta. \end{array} \right\}$

   'Only Mr. Tanaka didn't come. / Only Mr. Tanaka came.'

Shika, moreover, focuses on the non-existence or *lack* of an object or state, while *dake* emphasizes the unique existence of an object or a state. So, in (1), the fact that other people did not come is emphasized. In (2), on the other hand, the fact that Tanaka came is emphasized.

(3) 百円しかありません。

   Hyakuen shika arimasen.

   'I only have a hundred yen.'

(4) 百円だけあります。

   Hyakuen dake arimasu.

   'I have just a hundred yen.'

(3) focuses on the lack of money. Hence (3) is appropriate in giving reasons why the speaker cannot go to the movie, as in (5).

(5)
$$\left\{ \begin{array}{l} \text{百円しかありません} \\ {}^*\text{百円だけあります} \end{array} \right\} \text{から，映画へ行けません。}$$

$$\left\{ \begin{array}{l} \textit{Hyakuen shika arimasen} \\ {}^*\textit{Hyakuen dake arimasu} \end{array} \right\} \textit{kara, eiga e ikemasen.}$$

'I only have a hundred yen, so I cannot go to the movie.'

Lack of necessary money is a good reason why one cannot go to the movie but the existence of money is not.

Shika, therefore, is generally used when *more* is expected. No such expectation is felt with *dake*.

(6) 一問しか間違っていなかった。
Ichi-mon shika machigatte inakatta.
'There was only one mistake.'

(7) 一問だけ間違っていた。
Ichi-mon dake machigatte ita.
'There was just one mistake.'

(6) would be appropriate when one generally makes lots of mistakes or when one expected to have made lots of mistakes. (6) would be inappropriate in talking to a student who generally gets a hundred percent on tests. In such a case, (7) should be used.

27. WA vs. GA

1. Topic *wa*

The most important function of *wa* is to mark the *topic* of the sentence. The topic is a word or a group of words which indicates what the sentence is about. The speaker can introduce a noun phrase as a topic of the sentence when he can assume that the hearer can identify what it refers to either from the previous utterance, the context, or from general knowledge. A topic can be one of the following :

A. Nouns which have been mentioned in the previous discourse.

(1) きのう男の人が家へ来ました。その男の人は黒いぼうしをかぶっていました。

Kinoo otoko no hito ga uchi e kimashita. Sono otoko no hito wa kuroi booshi o kabutte imashita.

'A man came to the house yesterday. The man had a black hat on.'

B. Nouns which have not been mentioned in the previous discourse but can be inferred from the previous discourse.

(2) 先週車を買いました。エンジンは日本製です。

Senshuu kuruma o kaimashita. Enjin wa nihonsei desu.

'I bought a car yesterday. The engine was made in Japan.'

C. Nouns which can be identified non-linguistically.

(3) これは私の本です。

Kore wa watashi no hon desu.

'This is my book.'

D. Nouns which are uniquely identifiable, such as proper names, the sun, the moon, etc.

(4) アマゾン川は南アメリカにある。

Amazon-gawa wa minami amerika ni aru.

'The River Amazon is in South America.'

E. Generic Nouns

(5) 日本人はすしを食べる。

Nihonjin wa sushi o taberu.

'Japanese eat sushi.'

A topic phrase is generally placed at the beginning of the sentence. Any noun phrase in a sentence can become a topic.

(6) 田中さんは寝ています。

Tanaka-san wa nete imasu.

'Mr. Tanaka is sleeping.' (Subject is the topic.)

(7) この本はあの本屋で買いました。

Kono hon wa ano honya de kaimashita.

'As for this book, I bought it at that bookstore.' (Object is the topic.)

(8) あの喫茶店ではコーヒーを飲んだ。

Ano kissaten de wa, koohii o nonda.

'As for that coffee shop, I had coffee (there).' (Locative is the topic.)

2. Contrastive *wa*

Wa also indicates contrast.

(9) きのうは行きましたが、今日は行きません。

Kinoo wa ikimashita ga, kyoo wa ikimasen.

'I went yesterday, but I won't go today.'

(10) 田中さんは来ましたが、山川さんは来ませんでした。

Tanaka-san wa kimashita ga, Yamakawa-san wa kimasendeshita.

'Mr. Tanaka came, but Mr. Yamakawa did not come.'

Wa in negative sentences usually indicates *contrast*.

(11) ビールは飲みません。

Biiru wa nomimasen.

'I don't drink beer. (But, I drink something else.)'

(12) 学校へは行きませんでした。

Gakkoo e wa ikimasendeshita.

'I didn't go to school. (But, I went somewhere else.)'

Wa attached to adverbs and verbs are always *contrastive*.

(13) 上手には話せません。

Joozu ni wa hanasemasen.

'I can't speak well, (but I can speak somewhat.)'

(14) 田中さんと会いはしなかった。

Tanaka-san to ai wa shinakatta.

'I didn't meet with Mr. Tanaka, (but I talked to him).'

3. *Ga*

Ga marks the *subject* of the sentence. If what the subject NP refers to has not been mentioned in the previous discourse—i.e., is brought to the hearer's attention for the first time—*ga* should be used. So, in (1), *otoko no hito* is introduced into the discourse by *ga*. Once it is introduced into the discourse, it can then become a topic.

Kuno (1973) distinguishes two functions of *ga* for subject marking—exhaustive listing vs. neutral description.

A. *Ga* of Exhaustive listing

(15) 私がやりました。

Watashi ga yarimashita.

'*I* did (it).'

Ga of Exhaustive listing is used when one wants to convey the sense of 'it is X that ....' or 'X and only X ....' So, in (15), it is understood that someone did it. The question here is "who" did it.

B. *Ga* of Neutral description

(16) 雨が降っています。

Ame ga futte imasu.

'It is raining.'

(17) 男の人が立っています。

Otoko no hito ga tatte imasu.

'A man is standing.'

Ga is used here to bring an observable fact to the hearer's attention. So, (16) is not used to say that it is rain (and nothing else) that is coming down. (16) simply describes a scene of raining. (17) describes a scene of a man standing.

Another very important fact about *ga* is that the subjects of subordinate sentences are generally marked by *ga*. It is very important for students of Japanese to note that the topic *wa* does not appear in subordinate clauses.

(18) 父が来た時，私はいなかった。

Chichi ga kita toki, watashi wa inakatta.

'I was not (at home) when my father came.'

(19) 田中さんが買った本は日本の小説です。

Tanaka-san ga katta hon wa nihon no shoosetsu desu.

'The book Mr. Tanaka bought was a Japanese novel.'

(20) 子供が寝ているから，勉強をします。

Kodomo ga nete iru kara, benkyoo o shimasu.

'Because my child is sleeping, I will study.'

4 . *Wa* vs. *Ga*

As we have seen, in [X wa Y], X is something which has already been mentioned or implied in the context. Hence, *wa* directs the hearer's attention to what *follows* (i.e., Y). *Ga*, on the other hand, is used when the speaker wants to direct the hearer's attention to what precedes (i.e., X). Compare the following.

(21) 田中さんは学生です。

Tanaka-san wa gakusei desu.

'Mr. Tanaka is a student.'

Both the speaker and the hearer know who Mr. Tanaka is. What the speaker wants to convey is *what* he is—i.e., that he is *a student*.

This would be an answer to a question, e.g., "*Tanaka-san wa nan desu ka.*"

⑵ 田中さんが学生です。

Tanaka-san ga gakusei desu.

'It is Mr. Tanaka who is the student.'

The speaker wants to direct the hearer's attention to Mr. Tanaka. They know that someone is a student. The sentence tells *who* the student is. This would be an answer to a question "*Dare ga gakusei desu ka?*" This is a case of GA of exhaustive listing.

⑶ 漢字は難しいです。

Kanji wa muzukashii desu.

'As for Kanji, it is difficult.'

⑷ 漢字が難しいです。

Kanji ga muzukashii desu.

'*Kanji* is difficult. (It is kanji that is difficult.)'

In ⑶, the speaker is commenting on what *kanji* is like, while, in ⑷, one is defining *what* is difficult.

⑸ 駅はあそこにあります。

Eki wa asoko ni arimasu.

'The station is there.'

⑹ この辺に駅がありますか。

Kono hen ni eki ga arimasu ka?

'Is there any station nearby?'

In ⑸, the focus is on *where* the station is. In ⑹, the focus is on whether or not there is any station nearby. (This is a GA of neutral description.)

⑺ 試験はあしたですか。

Shiken wa ashita desu ka?

'Is the exam tomorrow?'

The focus is on *when* the exam is to be held.

(28) あした試験がありますか。

Asita shiken ga arimasu ka ?

'Is there an exam tomorrow?'

The speaker is interested in finding out if there is any exam tomorrow or not.

(29) 山川さんは今寝ています。

Yamakawa-san wa ima nete imasu.

'Mr. Yamakawa is sleeping right now.'

The speaker is interested in finding out what Mr. Yamakawa is doing right now.

(30) 山川さんが寝ています。

Yamakawa-san ga nete imasu.

a) 'Look! Mr. Yamakawa is sleeping!'

b) 'It is Mr. Yamakawa who is sleeping.'

This sentence is ambiguous. In one case, *ga* is interpreted as that of neutral description——i.e., the speaker comes into a place and finds out that Mr. Yamakawa is sleeping. In the other case, *ga* is interpreted as that of exhaustive listing——i.e., it is Mr. Yamakawa and nobody else who is sleeping.

(31) きのう男の人が来ました。その男の人は黒いコートを着ていました。

Kinoo otoko no hito ga kimashita. Sono otoko no hito wa kuroi kooto o kite imashita.

'A man came yesterday. The man had a black coat on.'

The first instance of '*otoko no hito*' is marked by *ga* since it is the

first time this phrase is mentioned in this conversation. The second
instance of '*otoko no hito*' is marked by *wa* because the phrase has
already been mentioned.

(32)　私は学生です。父は貿易会社に勤めています。

*Watashi wa gakusei desu. Chichi wa booeki-gaisha ni
tsutomete imasu.*

'I am a student. My father works for the import-export company.'

In this case, although '*chichi*' has not been mentioned before, *wa*
should be used, since '*chichi*' can be inferred from '*watashi*'. Once
'*watashi*' is mentioned, all the family members of '*watashi*' are
automatically registered in the discourse by inference.

As we noted earlier, one should pay special attention to the fact
that the subject of the subordinate clauses is generally marked by *Ga*.
Note the following contrast.

(33)　a.　子供が病気だから学校へ行けません。

Kodomo ga byooki da kara gakkoo e ikemasen.

'I can't go to school because my child is sick.'

　　　b.　子供は病気だから学校へ行けません。

Kodomo wa byooki da kara gakkoo e ikemasen.

'My child can't go to school because he/she is sick.'

Ga in (33a) makes it clear that *kodomo* is the subject of the *kara*
clause, but not the main clause. The use of *wa*, as in (33b),
however, indicates that *kodomo* is the subject of the main clause, as
well as the *kara* clause. The following are similar examples.

(34)　a.　父が帰って来てから御飯を作ります。

Chichi ga kaette kite kara gohan o tsukurimasu.

'I will prepare dinner after father returns home.'

　　　b.　父は帰って来てから御飯を作ります。

Chichi wa kaette kite kara gohan o tsukurimasu.
'Father prepares dinner after (he) returns home.'

Again, the person who cooks in (34a) is "the speaker" while it is "the father" in (34b).

BIBLIOGRAPHY

Alfonso (1966), Inoue (1983), Kuno (1973)

28. *WA* vs. *MO*

The particle *wa* indicates 'contrast' while *mo* indicates similarity. These particles can be used with numerical figures also. Consider the following.

   (1)   a . 太郎は十時間も寝ました。
          Taroo wa juujikan mo nemashita.
          'Taroo slept for as much as ten hours.'
      b . 太郎は十時間は寝ました。
          Taroo wa juujikan wa nemashita.
          'Taroo slept at least for ten hours.'

In (1a), the speaker thinks ten hours is a long time to sleep, thus the sense of 'as much as.' In (1b), Taroo slept at least for ten hours ; he could have slept more.

When the sentences are negated, both *mo* and *wa* present ambiguous interpretations. Consider the following.

   (2) 太郎は十時間も寝ませんでした。
      Taroo wa juujikan mo nemasendeshita.
      a . Taroo did not sleep for the duration of ten hours.
      b . Taroo slept for less than ten hours.

(3) 太郎は十時間は寝ませんでした。

Taroo wa juujikan wa nemasendeshita.

　a. Taroo did not sleep for the duration of at least ten hours.

　b. Taroo slept for less than ten hours.

Sentences (2) and (3) can both be an answer to a question such as (4).

(4) 太郎はきのう寝なかったでしょう。どのぐらい寝なかった
んですか。

*Taroo wa kinoo nenakatta deshoo. Dono gurai nena-
katta n desu ka ?*

'Taroo did not sleep last night, did he ? How long did he stay
up ?'

　a. 十時間も寝ませんでした。

Juujikan mo nemasendeshita.

'He did not sleep for as much as ten hours.'

　b. 十時間は寝ませんでした。

Juujikan wa nemasendeshita.

'He did not sleep for at least ten hours.'

Sentence (4) presupposes that Taroo did not sleep. *Mo* introduces
ten hours as a large figure. *Wa* introduces ten hours as a lower end
figure——it could have been more.

(5) 太郎はきのうどのぐらい寝ましたか。十時間ぐらいですか。

*Taroo wa kinoo dono gurai nemashita ka ? Juujikan
gurai desu ka ?*

'How long did Taroo sleep last night ? About ten hours ?'

　a. いいえ，十時間も寝ませんでした。

Iie, juujikan mo nemasendeshita.

'No, he did not sleep for ten hours.'

　b. いいえ，十時間は寝ませんでした。

Iie, juujikan wa nemasendeshita.

'No, he did not sleep for ten hours.'

Sentence (5) presupposes that Taroo slept. Both (5a) and (5b) imply that he slept less than ten hours. Here again, when *mo* is used, ten hours is presented as a surprisingly large number.

BIBLIOGRAPHY

Soga (1976)

SENTENCE-FINAL EXPRESSIONS

29. *N DESU* vs. *DESU/MASU* ─────────────────

The basic function of *n(o) desu* is to mark certain information as *known* in the context of a discourse. By using *no desu,* the speaker can present information which is known only to the speaker or the hearer *as if* it were *shared* information. The actual effect, however, varies considerably depending on the sentence types.

1 . Explanation

N(o) desu, in a statement, is often used to indicate an *explanation* for what the speaker has said or done or the state he is in.

(1) きのうは休みました。頭が痛かったんです。

Kinoo wa yasumimashita. Atama ga itakatta n desu.

'I was absent yesterday. (It is that) I had a headache.'

(2) ちょっとオフィスへ来て下さい。話があるんです。

Chotto ofisu e kite kudasai. Hanashi ga aru n desu.

'Please come to my office for a minute. (It is that) I have something to tell you.'

(3) a . どうしたんですか。

Doo shita n desu ka ?

'What happened ?'

b . おなかが痛いんです。

Onaka ga itai n desu.

'(It is that) I have a stomachache.'

In (1) and (2), Sentence + *n desu* offers an explanation for the preceding sentence. In (3), Sentence + *n desu* offers an explanation for the way the speaker of (3b) looks.

2 . Conjecture

When *n desu* is used in questions or in *deshoo* constructions, *n desu* is used to express one's conjectures on the basis of what one heard or observed.

(4)　a．雨が降っているんですか。

　　　Ame ga futte iru n desu ka ?

　　　'Is it that it is raining ?'

　　b．雨が降っていますか。

　　　Ame ga futte imasu ka ?

　　　'Is it raining ?'

(4a) is said only when there is a situation which makes one think that it might be raining (e. g., when one observes that somebody has a wet umbrella).　(4b) is a neutral question and is said when there is no basis for making any conjecture.

(5)　a．パーティーへ行くんですか。

　　　Paatii e iku n desu ka ?

　　　'Is it that you are going to the party ?'

　　b．パーティーへ行きますか。

　　　Paatii e ikimasu ka ?

　　　'Are you going to the party ?'

(5b) would be uttered when one wants to know if someone is going to the party or not.　(5a), on the other hand, will be uttered, for example, when one sees someone all dressed up as if he/she is going to the party.

So, in neutral information-seeking questions where there is no evidence with regard to what might be the case, as in (6), *do not* use *n desu ka.*

(6) もしもし，田中さんは $\left\{ \begin{array}{l} いますか。 \\ *いるんですか。 \end{array} \right\}$

    Moshi moshi, Tanaka san wa $\left\{ \begin{array}{l} \textit{imasu ka ?} \\ \textit{*iru n desu ka ?} \end{array} \right\}$

    'Hello. Is Mr. Tanaka there ?'

3 . Rapport

Frequently, in statements, *n(o) desu* is used in a context where there is no obvious situation to explain or conjecture about.

(7) 駅を出ると，大きな門が $\left\{ \begin{array}{ll} a . & あります。 \\ b . & あるんです。 \end{array} \right\}$ その門を通って，ちょっと歩くと，今度は左手に大きな杉の木が $\left\{ \begin{array}{ll} a . & あります。 \\ b . & あるんです。 \end{array} \right\}$

    Eki o deru to, ookina mon ga $\left\{ \begin{array}{ll} a . & \textit{arimasu.} \\ b . & \textit{aru n desu.} \end{array} \right\}$ *Sono mon o tootte, chotto aruku to, kondo wa hidarite ni ookina sugi no ki ga* $\left\{ \begin{array}{ll} a . & \textit{arimasu.} \\ b . & \textit{aru n desu.} \end{array} \right\}$

    'When you go out of the station, there is a large gate. Pass the gate and walk a little; then you will see a large cedar tree on the left.'

If one is giving directions on how to get somewhere, one would use (7a)——without *n desu*. If one is describing what one did, for example, one would use (7b)——sentences with *n desu*. The effect of *n desu* here is to create rapport with the hearer. By using *n desu*, the speaker tries to involve the hearer in the conversation or the speaker's point of view. This use of *n desu* resembles English 'you know' in conversation. (8) is another example.

(8)　a．そうです。

　　　　Soo desu.

　　　　'That's right.'

　　　b．そうなんです。

　　　　Soo na n desu.

　　　　'That's *right*.'

Sentence (8a) can be an answer to a question such as "*Anata wa gakusei desu ka*?" It simply acknowledges that the addressee's assumption is correct. Sentence (8b), on the other hand, shows the speaker's strong emotional involvement/rapport with the addressee.

4．Reproach

　　When *n desu* is used in *kara* 'because' clause, it often carries a reproachful tone.

(9)　お金が $\left\{ \begin{array}{l} a．ないんだ \\ b．ない \end{array} \right\}$ から無駄使いをしないで下さい。

　　　Okane ga $\left\{ \begin{array}{l} a．\text{\textit{nai n da}} \\ b．\text{\textit{nai}} \end{array} \right\}$ *kara mudazukai o shinaide*

　　　kudasai.

　　　'We don't have money. So, please don't waste it.'

(10)　きのう $\left\{ \begin{array}{l} a．行ったんだから \\ b．行ったから \end{array} \right\}$ 今日は行きません。

　　　Kinoo $\left\{ \begin{array}{l} a．\text{\textit{itta n da kara}} \\ b．\text{\textit{itta kara}} \end{array} \right\}$ *kyoo wa ikimasen.*

　　　'Since I went yesterday, I am not going today.'

Sentences (9b) and (10b) are neutral statements. When *n desu* is used as in (9a) and (10a), the statements bear a critical or reproachful tone. The speaker suggests that the hearer should have known the fact, for example, that they don't have money (in (9)) or the fact that the speaker went out (in (10))——the hearer should have known better.

5 . Backgrounding

N(o) desu is often used in *n desu ga, n desu ke(re)do,* as in (11) and (12).

(11) あしたパーティーがあるんですけど，来ませんか。
Ashita paatii ga aru n desu kedo, kimasen ka ?
'We are having a party tomorrow. Won't you come ?'

(12) あのレストランへは一度行ったことがあるんですが，とても良かったですよ。
Ano resutoran e wa ichido itta koto ga aru n desu ga,
totemo yokatta desu yo.
'I have been to that restaurant once, and it was very nice.'

By marking information as known in the context of discourse, *n desu* here indicates that the information introduced by *n desu* is subordinate in importance to what follows. It provides background information for what follows.

As we have seen, the effect of using *n(o) desu* varies considerably. In many cases, the use of *n(o) desu* makes one's speech sound softer and more polite, but one should be careful, since, in some situations, it can be quite offensive to the hearer.

Sentences (9) and (10) are such examples. (13) is another such example.

(13) A：私がやりましょうか。
Watashi ga yarimashoo ka ?
'Shall I do it ?'
B：a. いえ，私がやります。
Ie, watashi ga yarimasu.
'No, I will do it.'
b. いえ，私がやるんです。
Ie, watashi ga yaru n desu.
'No, I am going to do it.'

93

In a situation where there is some job to be done and A offers to do it, (13a) is an appropriate response. (13b), however, would be quite offensive to A because the use of *n desu* here implies that it has been decided that "I am going to do it" and the hearer should have known this.

> **BIBLIOGRAPHY**
> Kuno (1973), Alfonso (1966), McGloin (1980), Kunihiro (1984)

30. *NE* vs. *YO*

Sentence-final particles *yo* and *ne* give different force to statements. By using *ne*, the speaker seeks agreement or confirmation from the hearer, and as such *ne* is generally attached to information which the hearer can confirm. Observe the following.

(1) 今日はいいお天気ですね(え)。
Kyoo wa ii o-tenki desu ne(e).
'It's nice weather, isn't it.'

(2) お宅は渋谷でしたね。
Otaku wa Shibuya deshita ne.
'Your house is in Shibuya, right?'

In (1) and (2), both the speaker and the hearer know this piece of information. In (1), the speaker is seeking agreement from the hearer, and in (2), the speaker expects the hearer to confirm this information. The use of *ne* in (1) and (2) is very similar to the English tag-questions.

Ne, moreover, is also often used when the information is not known to the hearer, as in the following examples.

(3) 私は，肉がきらいなんですよね。

Watashi wa niku ga kírai na n desu yo ne.

'I don't like meat, you know.'

(4) 本当に困りましたね。あの時は。

Hontoo ni komarimashita ne. Ano toki wa.

'I was really in trouble then, you know.'

Suppose one is talking about one's likes and dislikes or one's past experience. Generally, this information is not known to the hearer, and hence the hearer cannot confirm it. The use of *ne* in (3) and (4), then, is to create an atmosphere of rapport with the hearer.

Yo, on the other hand, is used to insist on one's assertion, to impose some information on the hearer. Hence, *yo* is attached, in general, to the information which is known only to the speaker.

(5) さっき田中さんが来たよ。

Sakki Tanaka-san ga kita yo.

'Mr. Tanaka came a while ago.'

(6) 呼んでるよ。

Yonderu yo.

'(She) is calling you.'

In (5), the hearer does not know that Tanaka came. In (6), the speaker is calling to the hearer's attention a fact that the hearer was not aware of——i.e., that he was being called.

Used with statements, *yo* imposes an assertion as a claim, advice, warning, etc. One should be careful in using *yo*, especially in talking to social superiors, since the use of *yo* would be too imposing and hence impolite to one's superior. Observe the following conversation.

95

(7)　Teacher：日本でどこに住んでいましたか。

　　　　　　　Nihon de doko ni sunde imashita ka ?

　　　　　　　'Where did you live in Japan ?'

　　　Student：鎌倉に住んでいました。

　　　　　　　Kamakura ni sunde imashita.

　　　　　　　'I lived in Kamakura.'

　　　Teacher：鎌倉は，いいところですね。

　　　　　　　Kamakura wa ii tokoro desu ne.

　　　　　　　'Kamakura is a nice place, isn't it ?'

　　　Student：ええ。大仏も $\left\{ \begin{array}{l} {}^{??}ありますよ。\\ あります。 \end{array} \right\}$

　　　　　　　Ee. Daibutsu mo $\left\{ \begin{array}{l} {}^{??}arimasu\ yo.\\ arimasu. \end{array} \right\}$

　　　　　　　'Yes. There is a big Buddha also.'

(8)　Teacher：兄弟は何人ですか。

　　　　　　　Kyoodai wa nan-nin desu ka ?

　　　　　　　'How many siblings do you have ?'

　　　Student：$\left\{ \begin{array}{l} {}^{*}五人ですよ。\\ 五人です。 \end{array} \right\}$

　　　　　　　$\left\{ \begin{array}{l} {}^{*}Gonin\ desu\ yo.\\ Gonin\ desu. \end{array} \right\}$

　　　　　　　'I have five siblings.'

In (7), *yo* is impolite since the student presumes a lack of knowledge on the part of the teacher while presumably the teacher knows the fact. (8) is a neutral, information-seeking question and answer interchange. The use of *yo* is again too imposing and hence inappropriate. The use of *yo* is often argumentative, and hence students should be careful not to overuse the particle *yo*.

BIBLIOGRAPHY
Uyeno (1971)

31. *WAKE DE WA NAI* vs. *WAKE NI WA IKANAI* ——————

In the following examples, *wake de wa nai* and *wake ni wa ikanai* are both acceptable.

(1) 日本語を五年勉強していますが，日本人と同じように日本
語が書ける { a. 訳ではありません。 }
{ b. という訳にはいきません。 }

Nihongo o gonen benkyoo shite imasu ga, nihonjin to onaji yoo

ni nihongo ga kakeru { a. *wake de wa arimasen.* }
{ b. *toyuu wake ni wa iki-* }
{ *masen.* }

'I have been studying Japanese for five years, but that does not mean that I can write Japanese like native Japapanese.'

(2) 中国語が分かれば日本語が話せるという
{ a. 訳ではありません。 }
{ b. 訳にはいきません。 }

Chuugokugo ga wakareba nihongo ga hanaseru toyuu

{ a. *wake de wa arimasen.* }
{ b. *wake ni wa ikimasen.* }

'Just because you know Chinese does not mean you can speak Japanese.'

Basically, *wake de wa arimasen* means 'it does not logically follow.' So, if X is true, then Y usually (generally, logically) follows as a conclusion. *Wake de wa nai* negates this logical conclusion. *Wake ni wa ikanai* has the basic meaning of 'not possible due to social, moral or situational factors.' So,

(3) いくら暇だと言っても遊んでばかりいる
{ a. 訳ではない。 }
{ b. 訳にはいかない。 }

Ikura hima da to ittemo asonde bakari iru

$$\left\{ \begin{array}{l} a. \textit{ wake de wa nai.} \\ b. \textit{ wake ni wa ikanai.} \end{array} \right\}$$

'No matter how much free time I have, that does not mean that
I am just playing around.'

One generally deduces that if one has a lot of free time, one spends
time playing.　(3a) is a factual statement, which negates this conclusion, saying that (he) does not spend all his time playing around ; he
does other things.　Sentence (3b) is a more subjective statement.
Here, the speaker implies that he is obliged to do otherwise (not play
in (3)) because of social or moral reasons.

An objective/subjective difference holds for (1) and (2) also.　(1a)
and (2a) are objective or factual statements.　(1b) and (2b) impose
a subjective evaluation——the speaker implies that it is unreasonable
to expect that one can write like a native Japanese after five years of
study (in (1b)) or it is unreasonable to expect that one can speak
Japanese just because one knows Chinese (in (2b)).

32. (*iku*)WAKE NI WA IKANAI vs. (*ik*) ENAI ————————

When you want to express the idea that you cannot go to the
movie because you have an exam the next day, you can say either (1)
or (2).

(1) あした試験があるから，今日映画を見に行けません。
    Ashita shiken ga aru kara, kyoo eiga o mini ikemasen.
    'Because I have an. exam tomorrow, I cannot go see a movie
    today.'

(2) あした試験があるから，今日映画を見に行く訳にはいきま
    せん。
    Ashita shiken ga aru kara, kyoo eiga o mini iku wake ni

wa ikimasen.

'Because I have an exam tomorrow, I cannot very well go see a movie today.'

While *reru/rareru* potential form can be used either when one does not have ability (intellectual or physical) to do something or when one cannot do something because of situational/social reasons, *wake ni wa ikanai* can only be used in the latter case. So,

(3)　a.　日本語は話せません。

　　　Nihongo wa hanasemasen.

　　　1.　'I do not have the ability.'

　　　2.　'I have been prohibited from speaking in Japanese.'

　　b.　日本語を話す訳にはいきません。

　　　Nihongo o hanasu wake ni wa ikimasen.

　　　'I have been prohibited from speaking in Japanese.'

Wake ni wa ikanai, moreover, has a connotation of "not being able to do something because of moral/social obligation."

(4)　皆が仕事をしているから，一人だけ早く帰る訳にはいきません。

　　Mina ga shigoto o shite iru kara, hitori dake hayaku kaeru wake ni wa ikimasen.

　　'Since everyone is working, I cannot very well go home early.'

(5)　これは父の本ですから，あなたに貸す訳にはいきません。

　　Kore wa chichi no hon desu kara, anata ni kasu wake ni wa ikimasen.

　　'Because this is my father's book, I cannot very well lend it to you.'

Sentence (4) implies that the speaker feels certain obligation not to go home early——it does not feel right to do so ; "I will feel bad if I do so." The regular potential form is more objective and simply denies the possibility.

33. *YOO* vs. *SOO*

(V, Adj-stem) *soo* like *yoo* is used to give certain inferences on the basis of direct observation. (Stem)-*soo*, however, only gives the speaker's impression upon seeing something.

(1) おいしそうです。
Oishi-soo desu.
'It looks delicious.'

(2) 雨が降りそうです。
Ame ga furi-soo desu.
'It looks like it's going to rain.'

Sentence (1) states the speaker's impression of how a dish looks or smells. It might be truly tasty or it might turn out not to be tasty. Sentence (2) can be said by someone who looks out at the cloudy sky and feels that it is going to rain.

Yoo, on the other hand, involves more reasoning on the part of the speaker and hence the speaker is more committed to the truth of the proposition.

(3) この試験は難しそうだ。
Kono shiken wa muzukashi-soo da.
'This exam looks difficult.'

(4) この試験は難しいようだ。
Kono shiken wa muzukashii yoo da.
'It seems that this exam is difficult.'

Sentence (3) might be said by a student who just received an exam in giving his first impression about the exam. The exam looks difficult because it is long, it is written in small letters, etc. The speaker is not committed to the actual truth of the proposition. The test might turn out to be difficult or it might turn out to be easy. Sentence (4), on the other hand, might be said by a teacher who is giving an exam. Upon observing that the students are having trouble finishing the exam or showing signs of frustration, he conjectures that it might be difficult.

Some more examples follow :

(5) a . あの先生は親切そうですよ。

Ano sensei wa shinsetsu soo desu yo.

'(I met the teacher yesterday and) he looks like a nice person.)'

b . あの先生は親切なようですよ。

Ano sensei wa shinsetsu na yoo desu yo.

'It seems that he is a nice teacher. (I have some direct knowledge of how he behaves.)'

(6) a . かぜをひきそうです。

Kaze o hiki-soo desu.

'I feel like I am going to catch cold.'

b . かぜをひいたようです。

Kaze o hiita yoo desu.

'I seem to have caught cold. (I am sneezing, coughing, etc.)'

34. *YOO* vs. *RASHII*

Both *rashii* and *yoo* can be used to give conjectures, as in the following examples.

(1) 試験は難しかったようだ。

Shiken wa muzukashikatta yoo da.

'It looks like the exam was difficult.'

(2) 試験は難しかったらしい。

Shiken wa muzukashikatta rashii.

'It looks like the exam was difficult.'

With *yoo*, there is a sense that the conjecture is based on the speaker's first-hand information such as his/her *direct observation*. *Rashii*, on the other hand, gives a sense that the judgment is based on what one has *heard*. So, sentence (1) will be uttered, for example, by a teacher who has given an exam and observed that the students were having difficulty finishing it or were making grim faces, etc. Sentence (2), on the other hand, suggests that the speaker is basing his conjecture on what he has heard from someone.

(3) （あなたは）ちょっとやせたようですね。

（*Anata wa*) *chotto yaseta yoo desu ne.*

'It seems that you have lost a little weight.'

(4) （あなたは）ちょっとやせたらしいですね。

（*Anata wa*) *chotto yaseta rashii desu ne.*

'It seems that you have lost a little weight.'

Sentence (3), but not sentence (4), is appropriate when one sees somone and observes that he/she might have lost weight. Sentence (4) would be appropriate only when the speaker does not have firsthand information on how the addressee looks now but has heard from someone that the addressee has lost weight. One might say (4) on the telephone or by letter.

Yoo and *rashii* can also be used when there is no conjecture implied, as in the following.

(5) あの人は女のような人です。

Ano hito wa onna no yoo na hito desu.

'He is like a woman (i.e., he is effeminate).'

(6) あの人は女らしい人です。

Ano hito wa onna rashii hito desu.

'She is very feminine.'

In these cases—typically cases where *yoo* and *rashii* precede a noun, *yoo* is used to express a metaphor. So, in (5), the speaker knows that the person is not a woman (i.e., is a man). (5) states that that man looks or behaves like a woman. In (6), on the other hand, the speaker knows that the person is a woman. (6) states that that woman is truly feminine (i.e., has the true characteristics of a woman).

Similar examples are given.

(7) 今日は春のような日です。

Kyoo wa haru no yoo na hi desu.

'It's a spring-like day.'——You know it is not spring.

(8) 今日は春らしい日です。

Kyoo wa haru rashii hi desu.

'It's a typical spring day.'——You know it's spring.

(9) スミスさんは日本人のように日本語が上手です。

Sumisu-san wa nihonjin no yoo ni nihongo ga joozu desu.

'Mr. Smith speaks Japanese like a native.'——Mr. Smith is not Japanese.

Some sentences could imply either conjecture or non-conjecture.

(10) あれは魚のようですね。

Are wa sakana no yoo desu ne.

'That looks like a fish.'

(11) あれは魚らしいですよ。

Are wa sakana rashii desu yo.

'That seems to be a fish.'

Sentence (10) could mean : (i) one does not know exactly what it is but it looks like a fish ; or (ii) one knows that it is not a fish but it looks as if it were a fish.   Sentence (11) could mean either (i) one does not know exactly what it is but it seems that it is a fish; or (ii) one knows that it is a fish and it has the true characteristics of a fish.

| **BIBLIOGRAPHY**
Kashioka (1980)

NOUN PHRASES

35. *KOTO, NO* vs. *TO*

There are a number of verbs in Japanese which introduce the embedded sentence with either *koto/no* or *to*. When *koto* or *no* is used, the proposition introduced by *koto/no* is presupposed to be true by the speaker. *To*, on the other hand, simply reports what one heard, and thus there is no commitment on the part of the speaker as to the truth of the proposition. (Kuno 1973 : 213.)

(1) a. けんじは花子が結婚したと信じている。
   Kenji wa Hanako ga kekkon shita to shinjite iru.
   'Kenji believes that Hanako got married.'

   b. けんじは花子が結婚したことを信じない。
   Kenji wa Hanako ga kekkon shita koto o shinjinai.
   'Kenji does not believe the fact that Hanako got married.'

(2) a. 私はメリーが東京にいると聞いた。
   Watashi wa Merii ga Tookyoo ni iru to kiita.
   'I heard that Mary is in Tokyo.'

   b. 私はメリーが東京にいることを(つい最近まで)聞かなかった。
   Watashi wa Merii ga Tookyoo ni iru koto o (tsui saikin made) kikanakatta.
   'I did not hear (until recently) the fact that Mary is in Tokyo.'

In (1a), *to* indicates that Kenji believes that Hanako got married, but that might or might not be true. It is simply Kenji's belief.   In (1b), on the other hand, the speaker knows that it is a fact that Hanako got married and Kenji does not believe this fact.   Again in (2a), Mary might or might not be in Tokyo—this is what the speaker heard.   In (2b), the speaker presupposes it to be a fact that Mary is in Tokyo.

Hence, some verbs are always used with *to* and others only with *koto* or *no*.

(3)　a.　私はメリーが東京にいる {と / *ことを} 思った。

　　　　Watashi wa Merii ga Tookyoo ni iru {*to* / *koto o} *omotta.*

　　　　'I thought Mary was in Tokyo.'

　　b.　私はメリーが来た {と / *ことを} 早合点した。

　　　　Watashi wa Merii ga kita {*to* / *koto o} *hayagaten shita.*

　　　　'I jumped to the conclusion that Mary came.'

(4)　a.　私は花子が離婚した {ことを / のを / *と} 忘れていた。

　　　　Watashi wa Hanako ga rikon shita {*koto o* / *no o* / *to} *wasurete ita.*

　　　　'I forgot that Hanako got a divorce.'

　　b.　私は花子が碁が {上手な {ことを / のを} / *上手だと} 思い出した。

106

Watashi wa Hanako ga go ga

$$\left\{ \begin{array}{l} joozu\ na \left\{ \begin{array}{l} koto\ o \\ no\ o \end{array} \right\} \\ {}^{*}joozu\ da\ to \end{array} \right\} omoidashita.$$

'I remembered that Hanako is good at go.'

Verbs such as *omou*, *hayagatensuru*, by definition, pertain to one's belief, not a fact, and hence takes only *to*. However, one can forget or remember only what is considered to be a fact, and hence *to* is ungrammatical with verbs such as *wasureru*, *omoidasu*, etc.

Both *koto* and *no* are used with factual propositions. *No*, however, takes a more *concrete* proposition, while *koto* introduces a more *abstract* proposition.

No is used with verbs of sense perception, discovery, helping and stopping. They involve actions in which the subject directly perceives or directly responds to what's happening right then and there.

(5) a．私は花子が歩いて来る $\left\{ \begin{array}{l} のを \\ {}^{*}ことを \end{array} \right\}$ 見た。

　　Watashi wa Hanako ga aruite kuru $\left\{ \begin{array}{l} no\ o \\ {}^{*}koto\ o \end{array} \right\}$

　　mita.

'I saw Hanako walking toward me.' (sense perception)

　b．私は太郎がピアノをひいている $\left\{ \begin{array}{l} のを \\ {}^{*}ことを \end{array} \right\}$ 聞いた。

　　Watashi wa Taroo ga piano o hiite iru $\left\{ \begin{array}{l} no\ o \\ {}^{*}koto\ o \end{array} \right\}$

　　kiita.

'I heard Taroo playing the piano.' (sense perception)

　c．部屋に入って，子供がたばこを吸っている $\left\{ \begin{array}{l} のを \\ {}^{*}ことを \end{array} \right\}$

　　見つけた。

　　Heya ni haitte, kodomo ga tabako o sutte iru

$$\left\{ \begin{array}{c} no\ o \\ {}^{*}koto\ o \end{array} \right\} \ mitsuketa.$$

'I went into the room and found my child smoking.' (discovery)

d. 私は母が部屋を掃除する $\left\{ \begin{array}{c} のを \\ {}^{*}ことを \end{array} \right\}$ 手伝った。

Watashi wa haha ga heya o sooji suru $\left\{ \begin{array}{c} no\ o \\ {}^{*}koto\ o \end{array} \right\}$

tetsudatta.

'I helped my mother clean the room.' (helping)

e. 私は子供が外に出る $\left\{ \begin{array}{c} のを \\ {}^{*}ことを \end{array} \right\}$ 止めた。

Watashi wa kodomo ga soto ni deru $\left\{ \begin{array}{c} no\ o \\ {}^{*}koto\ o \end{array} \right\}$

tometa.

'I stopped my child from going out.' (stopping)

In (5), the situation is immediate and concrete.

Koto is used with verbs of learning, deduction, thinking, which involve an abstract process.

(6) a. コロンブスがアメリカを発見した $\left\{ \begin{array}{c} こと \\ {}^{*}の \end{array} \right\}$ を習った。

Koronbusu ga Amerika o hakken shita $\left\{ \begin{array}{c} koto \\ {}^{*}no \end{array} \right\}$ o

naratta.

'We learned that Columbus discovered America.'

b. アメリカの国土が日本の三十九倍もある $\left\{ \begin{array}{c} こと \\ {}^{*}の \end{array} \right\}$ を

考えてみて下さい。

Amerika no kokudo ga Nihon no sanjuu kyuu bai mo

aru $\left\{ \begin{array}{c} koto \\ {}^{*}no \end{array} \right\}$ o kangaete mite kudasai.

'Please consider the fact that America is 39 times as big as
Japan.'

c. 太郎は山田が犯人だった $\left\{ \begin{matrix} こと \\ *の \end{matrix} \right\}$ を正しく推定した。

Taroo wa Yamada ga han'nin datta $\left\{ \begin{matrix} koto \\ *no \end{matrix} \right\}$ *o*

tadashiku suitei shita.

'Taroo correctly inferred that Yamada was the culprit.'

So, examine the following sentences.

(7) a. 私はメリーがピアノをひくと聞いた。
       Watashi wa Merii ga piano o hiku to kiita.
       'I heard that Mary plays the piano.'

     b. 私はメリーがピアノをひくことを聞いた。
       Watashi wa Merii ga piano o hiku koto o kiita.
       'I heard that Mary plays the piano.'

     c. 私はメリーがピアノをひいているのを聞いた。
       Watashi wa Merii ga piano o hiite iru no o kiita.
       'I heard Mary playing the piano.'

In (7a), it might be a rumor that Mary plays the piano. In (7c), the
speaker heard Mary actually playing the piano. In (7b), the
speaker heard the news that Mary plays the piano, which the speaker
has reason to believe is true.

BIBLIOGRAPHY
Josephs (1976), Kuno (1973)

36. *KOTO, MONO* vs. *NO*

Koto and *no* are used as a noun meaning 'thing' and a pronoun meaning 'one', respectively. When used as a noun, *koto* still represents an abstract entity, such as subject matter, knowledge, etc., and thus should be clearly distinguished from *mono* which would represent concrete objects.

(1) いろいろな $\left\{\begin{matrix} こと \\ *もの \end{matrix}\right\}$ を習いました。

Iroiro na $\left\{\begin{matrix} koto \\ *mono \end{matrix}\right\}$ o naraimashita.

'I learned various things.'

(2) いろいろな $\left\{\begin{matrix} *こと \\ もの \end{matrix}\right\}$ を買いました。

Iroiro na $\left\{\begin{matrix} *koto \\ mono \end{matrix}\right\}$ o kaimashita.

'I bought many things.'

In the following example,

(3) a. 書きたいことがある。

Kakitai koto ga aru.

'I have something I want to write about.'

b. 書きたいものがある。

kakitai mono ga aru.

'I have something I want to write.'

koto represents an idea, a topic of writing, while *mono* represents an object such as a book.

No refers to both tangible and intangible objects, but does not generally refer to a highly abstract entity.

(4) a. 大きい車は高いが，小さいのは安い。

Ookii kuruma wa takai ga, chiisai no wa yasui.
'A big car is expensive, but a small one is cheap.'

b. 田中さんの意見はおもしろいが、山中さんのはちょっと問題がある。

Tanaka-san no iken wa omoshiroi ga, Yamanaka-san no wa chotto mondai ga aru.

'Mr. Tanaka's opinion is interesting, but there are problems with Mr. Yamanaka's.'

c. *日本の町人は経済的な力を持っていたが、政治的なのは持っていなかった。

**Nihon no choonin wa keizaiteki na chikara o motte ita ga, seijiteki na no wa motte inakatta.*

'Japanese merchants had economic power, but not political.'

When *no* is used to refer to people, moreover, it gives the connotation that people are treated as things. Hence, *no* can be used to refer to one's family member or a person whom one wants to put down, but not to someone to whom deference is due.

(5) お宅の御主人は、うちのとはできが違いますもの。

Otaku no goshujin wa uchi <u>no</u> to wa deki ga chigaimasu mono.

'My husband does not compare with yours.'

(6) *太郎の先生にはお会いしたけど、道子のにはまだお会いしていない。

**Taroo no sensei ni wa oai shita kedo, Michiko no ni wa mada oai shite inai.*

'I have met Taroo's teacher, but not Michiko's.'

BIBLIOGRAPHY
McGloin (1985)

37. SANNIN NO KODOMO (ga) vs. KODOMO (ga) SANNIN

Numerals often appear either before or after the nouns they modify, as in (1).

(1) a. 三人の子供がいるので，大変です。

       Sannin no kodomo ga iru node, taihen desu.

       'I have three children, and so it's a lot of work.'

   b. 子供が三人いるので，大変です。

       Kodomo ga sannin iru node, taihen desu.

       'I have three children, and so it's a lot of work.'

In example (1), it does not seem to make much difference whether a numeral comes before or after the noun.

In some contexts, however, one expression is preferred over the other.

(2) a. ᵗパーティーで五本のビールを飲んだ。

       ᵗ*Paatii de gohon no biiru o nonda.*

   b. パーティーでビールを五本飲んだ。

       Paatii de biiru o gohon nonda.

       'I drank five bottles of beer at the party.'

In some contexts, a clear difference in meaning can be observed between these two types of expressions.

(3) a. この三冊の本を下さい。

       Kono sansatsu no hon o kudasai.

   b. この本を三冊下さい。

       Kono hon o sansatsu kudasai.

(3a) suggests that the three books form a unit (e.g., trilogy). If one is buying three copies of one book, (3b) should be used.

Observe another example.

(4) a. 日本語を勉強している三人の学生を招待した。

    Nihongo o benkyoo shite iru sannin no gakusei o shootai shita.

    b. 日本語を勉強している学生を三人招待した。

    Nihongo o benkyoo shite iru gakusei o sannin shootai shita.

Sentence (4a) could mean (a) there are only three students who are studying Japanese and (the speaker) invited them, or (b) there are more than three students who are studying Japanese and (the speaker) invited three of them. Sentence (4b), on the other hand, has only the (b) reading.

So, when Numeral-Counter precedes a noun, there is a definite implication that the things or people under discussion are seen as a unit.

38. *SONO* vs. *ANO*

When the objects are physically present in the conversational context, the SO-series (*sono, sore, soko, sochira, sonna*) refers to an object which is closer to the hearer than the speaker. The A-series (*ano, are, asoko, achira, anna*) is used to refer to an object which is far from both the speaker and the hearer.

The SO-series, however, can also be used to refer to someone/ something that the speaker does not think the hearer knows or when the speaker does not know the referent. The A-series is used when the speaker thinks that both the speaker and the hearer know the referent. (Kuno 1973 : 283) Following are some examples.

(1)　A：きのうパーティーでスミスさんに会いましたよ。

　　　Kinoo paatii de sumisu-san ni aimashita yo.

　　　$\left\{\begin{array}{l}あの人\\ *その人\end{array}\right\}$ はいつも元気ですね。

　　　$\left\{\begin{array}{l}Ano\ hito\\ *Sono\ hito\end{array}\right\}$ *wa itsumo genki desu ne.*

　　　'Yesterday I met Mr. Smith at a party.　He is always well, isn't he ?'

　　　B：ほんとうに元気ですね。

　　　Hontoo ni genki desu ne.

　　　'Indeed, he is.'

(2)　A：きのうパーティーでスミスという人に会ったんですが，

　　　$\left\{\begin{array}{l}その人\\ *あの人\end{array}\right\}$ 一度山中さんに会いたいと言っていま

　　　したよ。

　　　Kinoo paatii de sumisu toyuu hito ni atta n desu ga,

　　　$\left\{\begin{array}{l}sono\ hito\\ *ano\ hito\end{array}\right\}$ *ichido yamanaka-san ni aitai to itte*

　　　imashita yo.

　　　'Yesterday I met someone by the name of Smith at a party. He said he would like to see you (Mr. Yamanaka) sometime.'

　　　B：そうですか。それで $\left\{\begin{array}{l}その人\\ *あの人\end{array}\right\}$ どんな人ですか。

　　　Soo desu ka.　Sorede, $\left\{\begin{array}{l}sono\ hito\\ *ano\ hito\end{array}\right\}$ *donna hito*

　　　desu ka ?

　　　'Oh, really ?　What kind of person is he ?'

In (1), Smith is known to both A and B, and hence *ano hito* is used.
In (2), Smith is known to A but not to B, and hence *sono hito* is used.
Following are similar examples.

(3)　A：きのう日光へ行ってきました。

　　　Kinoo Nikkoo e itte kimashita.

　　　'I went to Nikkoo yesterday.'

　　B：ああ、$\left\{\begin{array}{l}\text{あそこ}\\ *\text{そこ}\end{array}\right\}$はいいところですね。

　　　Aa, $\left\{\begin{array}{l} asoko \\ * soko \end{array}\right\}$ *wa ii tokoro desu ne.*

　　　'Oh, yes, that's a very nice place.'

(4)　A：きのう，みぞという所へ行ってきました。

　　　Kinoo, Mizo toyuu tokoro e itte kimashita.

　　　'I went to a place called Mizo yesterday.'

　　B：へえ，$\left\{\begin{array}{l}\text{そこ}\\ *\text{あそこ}\end{array}\right\}$はどこですか。

　　　Hee, $\left\{\begin{array}{l} soko \\ * asoko \end{array}\right\}$ *wa doko desu ka.*

　　　'Where is this place?'

(5)　A：「乱」という映画を見たことがありますか。

　　　"Ran" toyuu eiga o mita koto ga arimasu ka?

　　　'Have you seen a movie called "Ran"?'

　　B：ええ，$\left\{\begin{array}{l}\text{あれ}\\ *\text{それ}\end{array}\right\}$はいい映画ですね。

　　　Ee, $\left\{\begin{array}{l} are \\ * sore \end{array}\right\}$ *wa ii eiga desu ne.*

　　　'Yes.　That is a good movie.'

(6)　A：「乱」という映画を見たことがありますか。

　　　"Ran" toyuu eiga o mita koto ga arimasu ka?

　　　'Have you seen a movie called "Ran"?'

　　B：いいえ，$\left\{\begin{array}{l}*\text{あれ}\\ \text{それ}\end{array}\right\}$は誰が作った映画ですか。

　　　Iie, $\left\{\begin{array}{l} * are \\ sore \end{array}\right\}$ *wa dare ga tsukutta eiga desu ka?*

　　　'No.　Who directed the movie?'

In some cases, the *so*-series can be used even when the speaker knows that the referent is known to both the speaker and the hearer. Observe the following sentences.

(7) A：きのうパーティーで木村よし子という人に会いました
　　　　よ。専門は英語とか言っていましたが，とてもおも
　　　　しろい人でした。

　　*Kinoo paatii de Kimura Yoshiko toyuu hito ni ai-
　　mashita yo.　Senmon wa eigo toka itte imashita ga,
　　totemo omoshiroi hito deshita.*

　　'Yesterday, I met a person named Yoshiko Kimura at a
　　party.　She is majoring in English and is a very interest-
　　ing person.'

B：え，木村よし子？　{ その / あの } 人は私の同級生ですよ。

　　*E,　Kimura Yoshiko ?　{ Sono / Ano }　hito wa watashi
　　no dookyuusei desu yo.*
　　'You said Yoshiko Kimura ?　She is my classmate.'

In (7), speaker B discovers that he/she knows the person speaker A has been talking about.　Hence, speaker B can refer to her as *ano hito*.　Speaker B can also refer to the person as *sono hito*, indicating that it is the person *"you just mentioned"*.　When *sono* is used in such cases, the speaker wants to emphasize what has just been mentioned rather than the factual knowledge.

(8) A 1：二年前に習った今野先生を覚えてる？　ほら，ギャ
　　　　　ンブルは罪悪だと言った先生。

　　*Ninen mae ni naratta Konno sensei o oboeteru ?
　　Hora, gyanburu wa zaiaku da to itta sensei.*

　　'Do you remember Prof. Konno who taught us two years
　　ago ?　It's the teacher who said gambling is a sin.'

116

B： ええ。

Ee.

'Yes.'

A 2： $\left\{\begin{array}{c} あの \\ その \end{array}\right\}$ 今野先生が今じゃ競馬，競輪にこっている

んだよ。

$\left\{\begin{array}{c} Ano \\ Sono \end{array}\right\}$ *Konno sensei ga ima ja keiba, keirin ni*

kotte iru n da yo.

'That Prof. Konno is now totally absorbed in betting on horses and bicycle races.'

(Hinds 1973 : 6)

In (8), both speaker A and speaker B know the referent——Prof. Konno. In (8A2), either *ano* or *sono* is possible. When *sono* is used, however, the speaker puts an emphasis on what he has just said in (A1), thus putting an emphasis on the contrast between Prof. Konno, who said that gambling is bad, and the present Prof. Konno, who is absorbed in gambling.

In the narrative passage, where the narrator cannot assume shared knowledge with the reader, the use of the A-series should be avoided.

(9) 山本は日光の東照宮の近くに旅館を見つけて，

$\left\{\begin{array}{c} そこ \\ *あそこ \end{array}\right\}$ に泊まった。

Yamamoto wa Nikkoo no Tooshooguu no chikaku ni

ryokan o mitsukete, $\left\{\begin{array}{c} soko \\ *asoko \end{array}\right\}$ *ni tomatta.*

'Yamamoto found an inn near Tooshooguu temple and spent a night there.'

BIBLIOGRAPHY

Hinds (1973), Kuno (1973)

39. *TOYUU NO/KOTO* vs. *NO/KOTO*

Toyuu introduces contents of hearsay, report, rumor or the like. Hence, *toyuu* is obligatory with nouns of communications, as in (1) and (2).

(1) 花子が結婚したといううわさを聞いた。
   Hanako ga kekkon shita toyuu uwasa o kiita.
   'I heard the rumor that Hanako got married.'

(2) 子供が生まれたという知らせを受け取った。
   Kodomo ga umareta toyuu shirase o uketotta.
   'I received the news that a baby was born.'

Similarly *toyuu koto/toyuu no* often has the implication that what is said is hearsay or the claim of someone else.

(3) あなたが結婚した { というの / ?? の } は本当ですか。

   Anata ga kekkon shita { *toyuu no* / ?? *no* } *wa hontoo desu ka ?*

   'Is it true that you got married ?'

(4) 私が結婚した { というの / * の } はうそです。

   Watashi ga kekkon shita { *toyuu no* / * *no* } *wa uso desu.*

   'It is untrue that I got married.'

(5) 車があると便利だということは事実です。
   Kuruma ga aru to benri da toyuu koto wa jijitsu desu.
   'It is a fact that if you have a car, it is convenient.'

(6) 練習しなければ上手にならないということは確かです。
   Renshuu shinakereba joozu ni naranai toyuu koto wa tashika desu.

'It is true that you do not get better unless you practice.'

In (3), the speaker has heard that the addressee got married and asks if that is true. In (4), the speaker denies the truth of the report that he got married. In both (3) and (4), sentences without *toyuu* are not grammatical. If *toyuu* is absent in (3), it would imply that the speaker knows it to be a fact that the addressee got married, and in such case it would be inappropriate to ask if the fact is true. In (5) and (6), the speaker asserts to be true what is generally claimed by people——e.g., if one does not practice, one does not get better.

BIBLIOGRAPHY
Terakura (1983)

VERB PHRASES

40. *HOSHII* vs. *HOSHIGARU* ─────────────

It is well known that adjectives of desires (-*tai*, *hoshii*) and those of sensation (e.g., *sabishii*, *ureshii*, *kanashii*, etc.) require the first person subject in declarative sentences. The suffix -*garu* is required when the subject is in the third person.

(1)　a．私はカメラがほしい。

　　　　Watashi wa kamera ga hoshii.

　　　　'I want a camera.'

　　b．太郎はカメラをほしがっている。

　　　　Taroo wa kamera o hoshigatte iru.

　　　　'Taroo wants a camera.'

(2)　a．私はさびしい。

　　　　Watashi wa sabishii.

　　　　'I am sad.'

　　b．太郎はさびしがっている。

　　　　Taroo wa sabishigatte iru.

　　　　'Taroo is sad.'

We will refer to (a)-type as an "adjectival form" and (b)-type as a "verbal form." The suffix -*garu* means "to show a sign of", and as such a desire or sensation should be observable to someone other than the subject. Since the speaker cannot directly experience some-one else's feeling, it has to be described as the speaker's report/observation.

The adjectival form, however, does occur with the third person subject in some subordinate clauses (e.g., (3) and (4)) as well as when it precedes expressions such as *rashii, yoo da,* etc.

(3) 太郎は車がほしいから，アルバイトをしている。

    Taroo wa kuruma ga hoshii kara, arubaito o shite iru.

    'Taroo is working part-time because he wants a car.'

(4) 花子はさびしいのに，何も言わなかった。

    Hanako wa sabishii noni, nanimo iwanakatta.

    'Hanako was lonely, but she did not say anything.'

(5) メリーは日本へ行きたいらしい。

    Merii wa Nihon e ikitai rashii.

    'It seems like Mary wants to go to Japan.'

Now, compare the following sentences.

(6) 太郎は { 車がほしい / *車をほしがっている } から，アルバイトをしている。

    Taroo wa { *kuruma ga hoshii* / **kuruma o hoshigatte iru* } *kara, arubaito o shite iru.*

    'Taroo wants a car, and so he is working part-time.'

(7) 太郎が { *ほしい / ほしがっている } から，買ってやった。

    Taroo ga { *hoshii / *hoshigatte iru* } *kara, katte yatta.*

    'Because Taroo wants it, I bought it for him.'

The difference between (6) and (7) is the speaker's perspective. In (7), the speaker is an outside observer of Taroo, while, in (6), the speaker takes on Taroo's perspective and describes Taroo from within. In (6), Taroo asserts "*I* want a car", while, in (7), the speaker asserts "*Taroo* wants a car." Hence, an adjectival form in the former and a verbal form in the latter.

Similarly,

(8) a. メリーは日本へ行きたいそうだ。
     Merii wa Nihon e ikitai soo da.
     'I hear Mary wants to go to Japan.'

  b. メリーは日本へ行きたがっているそうだ。
     Merii wa Nihon e ikitagatte iru soo da.
     'I hear Mary wants to go to Japan.'

In (8a), Mary said "I want to go to Japan," and this is what the speaker is reporting. Hence, the *tai* form is used in (8a). In (8b), someone said, "Mary wants to go to Japan, " and this is what is reported by the speaker. Hence, *tagaru* is used in (8b).

41. *IRERU* vs. *HAIRASERU* ─────────────────────

There are many intransitive verbs which have corresponding transitive verbs such as *hairu* (intransitive)/*ireru*(transitive), *tomaru* (intr.)/*tomeru*(tr.), *noru*(intr.)/*noseru*(tr.), etc. For such intransitive-transitive verb pairs, the transitive pair and causative forms of the intransitive pair are very similar in meaning in that they both express the idea of causing some event to happen.

(1) a. 学生が部屋に入った。
     Gakusei ga heya ni haitta.
     'The students entered the room.'

  b. 先生は学生を部屋に入れた。
     Sensei wa gakusei o heya ni ireta.
     'The teacher put the students in the room.'

  c. 先生は学生を部屋に入らせた。

> *Sensei wa gakusei o heya ni hairaseta.*
> 'The teacher had the students enter the room.'

(2) a. お茶が入った。
> *Ocha ga haitta.*
> 'Tea is served.'

   b. 花子はお茶を入れた。
> *Hanako wa ocha o ireta.*
> 'Hanako served tea.'

   c. *花子はお茶を入らせた。
> **Hanako wa ocha o hairaseta.*

Both (1b) and (1c) express the idea of the teacher causing the students to enter the room. When the action pertains to an inanimate object as in (2), however, only the transitive verb construction is appropriate in a normal context.

In many cases, there is a clear division of labor between the transitive pair and the causative form of the intransitive pair. Observe the following sentences.

(3) a. 母親は子供をお風呂に入れた。
> *Hahaoya wa kodomo o ofuro ni ireta.*
> 'The mother bathed the child.'

   b. 母親は子供をお風呂に入らせた。
> *Hahaoya wa kodomo o ofuro ni hairaseta.*
> 'The mother had the child take a bath.'

(4) a. 母親は子供を寝かした。
> *Hahaoya wa kodomo o nekashita.*
> 'The mother put the child to bed.'

   b. 母親は子供を寝させた。
> *Hahaoya wa kodomo o nesaseta.*
> 'The mother let the child sleep.'

(5) a. 母親は子供に洋服を着せた。
> *Hahaoya wa kodomo ni yoofuku o kiseta.*

'The mother put clothes on the child.'

b. 母親は子供に洋服を着させた。

Hahaoya wa kodomo ni yoofuku o kisaseta.

'The mother had the child put on clothes.'

The transitive verbs in (3a)-(5a) generally imply that the person was *directly* involved in causing the event. In (3a), the mother literally bathed the child, putting him in a bathtub and washing him, etc. In (4a), the mother put the child to sleep by singing, tucking him/her in bed or the like. In (5a), the mother actually put the clothes on the child. Such direct physical involvement is not felt with causative forms of an intransitive pair. Sentences (3b)-(5b) strongly imply that the child did the actions himself and the mother simply caused the actions to happen, perhaps by telling the child to do so.

The use of a transitive pair, however, does not always suggest direct physical involvement. Observe the following sentences.

(6) a. 入れて下さい。

Irete kudasai.

'Please let me in.'

b. 入らせて下さい。

Hairasete kudasai.

'Please let me come in.'

(7) a. 太郎は花子を学校の前で降ろした。

Taroo wa Hanako o gakkoo no mae de oroshita.

'Taroo dropped Hanako off in front of the school.'

b. 太郎は花子を学校の前で降りさせた。

Taroo wa Hanako o gakkoo no mae de orisaseta.

'Taroo had Hanako get out of the car in front of the school.'

(8) a. 私は通行人を止めた。

Watashi wa tsuukoonin o tometa.

'I stopped the passerby.'

b. 私は通行人を止まらせた。

Watashi wa tsuukoonin o tomaraseta.
'I made the passerby stop.'

Ireru can be used when someone literally pushes someone else to get in somewhere, but no such use of force is felt in (6). In such a case, transitive pairs tend to be used when the causation is done in connection with some conventional or standard situations, while causative forms tend to be used in connection with non-standard situations. (Shibatani 1967 : 265.)

So, (6a) is preferred, for example, when a person wants to enter his own house or when a person wants to enter a movie theater in order to see a movie. (6b), on the other hand, could be used when the entering is wanted for a non-conventional purpose, such as a salesman wishing to enter the house or a person wanting to obtain temporary access to a building. (7a) can be used when Taroo brings Hanako to the school she attends. (7b) gives the sense that it was incidental that Taroo made Hanako get out of the car in front of the school (perhaps, Hanako was too noisy, perhaps they had a flat tire, etc.). Similarly, when one stops a passerby to ask for directions (i.e., a conventional purpose), (8a) but not (8b) would be used.

BIBLIOGRAPHY
Miyagawa (1984), Shibatani (1976)

42. *KOTO NI NARU/SURU* vs. *YOO NI NARU/SURU* ———

There are two basic differences involved in these expressions. One is the difference between *koto* and *yoo*. *Koto* implies that a certain *decision* has been made, while *yoo* indicates that a gradual *change* has taken place. So,

(1) a. たばこをやめることになりました。
     Tabako o yameru koto ni narimashita.
     'It has been decided that we will quit smoking.'
   b. たばこをやめるようになりました。
     Tabako o yameru yoo ni narimashita.
     'It has become such that people quit smoking.'

In (1a), with *koto*, it indicates that a certain decision (perhaps a legal one) has been made that people should quit smoking. No such decision is implied in (1b). Sentence (1b) simply points to a gradual change which took place——people gradually came to quit smoking.

Another distinction is that between *suru* and *naru*. *Suru* basically indicates that the subject of the sentence has control of an action, while *naru* indicates that the subject of the sentence is a passive recipient of some decision or some change. So,

(2) a. 日本へ行くことにしました。
     Nihon e iku koto ni shimashita.
     'I have decided that I will go to Japan.'
   b. 日本へ行くことになりました。
     Nihon e iku koto ni narimashita.
     'It has been decided that I will go to Japan.'

In (2a), the speaker actively made a decision to go to Japan, while, in (2b), the decision was made (by someone) for him.

Notice that in many cases, although the decision might have been made by the speaker himself, *koto ni naru* is used instead of *koto ni suru*, since it sounds more polite, more impersonal or more formal. Study the following examples.

(3) A：今晩一緒に食事に行きませんか。
     Konban issho ni shokuji ni ikimasen ka ?

'How about going out for dinner tonight ?'

B：今晩ですか。実はあいにく今晩は家内と出かけること
に $\left\{ \begin{array}{c} なって \\ *して \end{array} \right\}$ いるんですよ。

Konban desu ka ? Jitsu wa ainiku konban wa kanai

to dekakeru koto ni $\left\{ \begin{array}{c} natte \\ *shite \end{array} \right\}$ *iru n desu yo.*

'Tonight ? Unfortunately, I am supposed to have dinner with my wife.'

(4) A：この度，縁があって，結婚することになりました。

Kono tabi, en ga atte, kekkon suru koto ni nari mashita.

'I will be getting married soon.'

B：そうですか。それはおめでとうございます。

Soo desu ka . Sore wa omedetoo gozaimasu.

'Is that right ? Congratulations.'

In (3), it is possible that the speaker actually made a decision to go out with his wife. Using *ni naru*——i.e., by presenting it as if things have been already arranged for him——softens the statement, and hence makes his excuse sound more indirect and polite.

When these expressions are used in *-te iru* forms, it often indicates that a certain decision/change has become a rule or a habit.

(5) a . 毎日勉強することにしています。

Mainichi benkyoo suru koto ni shite imasu.

'I make it a rule to study everyday.'

b . 毎日勉強するようにしています。

Mainichi benkyoo suru yoo ni shite imasu.

'I make a point of studying everyday.'

The following summarizes the constructions involving *yoo ni/ koto ni naru/suru.*

(6) a. 毎日勉強することにします。

Mainichi benkyoo suru koto ni shimasu.

'I am going to (am deciding to) study everyday.'

b. 毎日勉強することにしています。

Mainichi benkyoo suru koto ni shite imasu.

'I make it a rule to study everyday.'

c. 毎日勉強することにしました。

Mainichi benkyoo suru koto ni shimashita.

'I have decided to study everyday.'

d. 毎日勉強することになるでしょう。

Mainichi benkyoo suru koto ni naru deshoo.

'It will be decided on/It will become a rule that we study everyday.'

e. 田中さんは朝一時間と夜三時間家で勉強します。毎日四時間勉強していることになります。

Tanaka-san wa asa ichijikan to yoru sanjikan uchi de benkyoo shimasu. Mainichi yojikan benkyoo shite iru koto ni narimasu.

'Mr. Tanaka studies one hour in the morning and three hours in the evening. That means he is studying four hours everyday.'

f. 毎日勉強することになっています。

Mainichi benkyoo suru koto ni natte imasu.

'It is a rule to study everyday.'

g. 毎日勉強することになりました。

Mainichi benkyoo suru koto ni narimashita.

'It has become a rule to study everyday.'

(7) a. これから毎日勉強するようにします。

Korekara mainichi benkyoo suru yoo ni shimasu.

'I will try to study everyday from now on.'

b. 毎日勉強するようにしています。

Mainichi benkyoo suru yoo ni shite imasu.

'I make an effort to study everyday.'

c. 毎日勉強するようにしました。

Mainichi benkyoo suru yoo ni shimashita.

'I made an effort to study everyday.'

d. (ほうびをやれば) 毎日勉強するようになります。

(*Hoobi o yareba*) *mainichi benkyoo suru yoo ni narimasu.*

'(If you give rewards,) they will come to study everyday.'

e. 日本の大学は入れば出られるようになっています。

Nihon no daigaku wa haireba derareru yoo ni natte imasu.

'Japanese universities are such that one can graduate once one gets in.'

f. このごろ毎日勉強するようになりました。

Konogoro mainichi benkyoo suru yoo ni narimashita.

'They have come to study everyday these days.'

43. *KURERU* VS. *AGERU*

There are two verbs which mean 'to give' in Japanese. Basically, when the giving is directed toward the speaker—i.e., when the receiver is the speaker, *kureru* is used.

In [X *ga* Y *ni* Z *o* (V-*te*) *kureru*], Y is either the speaker—me (or the hearer—you—in questions) or someone who is closer to the speaker than X in relationships.

(1) 花子が(私に)おかしをくれた。

Hanako ga (*watashi ni*) *okashi o kureta.*

'Hanako gave me a sweet.'

(2) 太郎が花子におかしをくれた。

Taroo ga Hanako ni okashi o kureta.
'Taroo gave Hanako a sweet.'

In (1), Y is the speaker. In (2), Hanako is someone who is closer to the speaker than Taroo. Hanako could be the speaker's sister and Taroo the speaker's friend.

The relationships among people can be briefly schematized as follows.

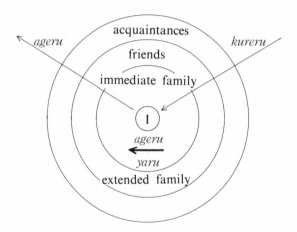

"I" the speaker is in the center of all relationships. When the giving is directed toward the speaker, *kureru* is used. When the giving is directed away from the speaker or when the giver and the receiver have about the same degree of closeness to the speaker, *ageru* (or *yaru*) is used.

(3) 私は姉にセーターを買ってあげた。
    Watashi wa ane ni seetaa o katte ageta.
    'I bought a sweater for my sister.'

(4) 姉は妹にレコードをやるつもりだ。
    Ane wa imooto ni rekoodo o yaru tsumori da.
    'My older sister is planning to give a record to my younger
      sister.'

When the speaker is asking a question or making a statement about the hearer, *kureru* is used if the giving is directed toward the hearer. In other words, in questions, the perspective shifts from the speaker to the hearer. (5A2) and (6A1) are such examples.

(5)　A1：クリスマスにお姉さんに何かあげましたか。

　　　Kurisumasu ni oneesan ni nanika agemashita ka ?

　　　'Did you give anything to your sister for Christmas ?'

　　B1：ええ，本をあげました。

　　　Ee, hon o agemashita.

　　　'Yes, I give her a book.'

　　A2：お姉さんも何かくれましたか。

　　　Oneesan mo nanika kuremashita ka ?

　　　'Did your sister give you something also ?'

　　B2：ええ，レコードをくれました。

　　　Ee, rekoodo o kuremashita.

　　　'Yes, she gave me a record.'

(6)　A1：お母さんはよくいろいろなものをくれますね。

　　　Okaasan wa yoku iroiro na mono o kuremasu ne.

　　　'Your mother gives you lots of things, doesn't she ?'

　　B1：ええ。

　　　Ee.

　　　'Yes.'

　　A2：あなたも何かあげますか。

　　　Anata mo nanika agemasu ka ?

　　　'Do you give her something too ?'

Even in questions, however, if the speaker (or someone whom the speaker considers as a member of his group) is the giver, *ageru* should be used. (7A2) is an example.

(7)　A1：田中さんは何をくれたの？

　　　Tanaka-san wa nani o kureta no ?

'What did Mr. Tanaka give you ?'

Ｂ１：本をくれた。

Hon o kureta.

'He gave me a book.'

Ａ２：うちの妹は何をあげた？

Uchi no imooto wa nani o ageta ?

'What did my sister give you ?'

Ｂ２：妹さんは音楽会の切符をくれた。

Imooto-san wa ongakukai no kippu o kureta.

'Your sister gave me a concert ticket.'

BIBLIOGRAPY

Kuno (1973, 1976)

44. *MAMA* vs. *-TE*

Verb(plain-past) + *mama* and verb-*te* form both express that two simultaneous situations hold at the same time. So, in the following sentences,

(1)　a．立ったまま話した。

Tatta mama hanashita.

'I talked standing.'

　　b．立って話した。

Tatte hanashita.

'I talked standing.'

the speaker was standing while he talked.

There are several differences between them, however. First, *mama* implies that the situation has existed for some time——(1a) implies that (he) has been standing prior to talking. In (1b), (he) could have been standing or (he) could have been sitting. In response to a question such as "Did you talk sitting down or standing up ?," (1b) would be appropriate.

Second, *mama* often implies that one should have done otherwise or at least that the norm is to do otherwise. So, (1a) implies that the person should have sat down but kept standing while he talked. Sentence (1b) does not carry such negative connotation.

Following are some more examples.

(2) a. 旗を持ったまま歩いた。
   Hata o motta mama aruita.
   'I walked carrying a flag.'

   b. 旗を持って歩いた。
   Hata o motte aruita.
   'I walked carrying a flag.'

(3) a. 帽子をかぶったまま入った。
   Booshi o kabutta mama haitta.
   'I entered (a room) with my hat on.'

   b. 帽子をかぶって入った。
   Booshi o kabutte haitta.
   'I entered (a room) with my hat on.'

Sentences (2a) and (3a) imply that one should have left the flag and that one should have taken his hat off, respectively.

45. *NAKEREBA NARANAI* vs. *NAKEREBA IKENAI* ─────────

Both V-*nakereba naranai* and V-*nakereba ikenai* express the sense of obligation.

(1) a. クラスでは日本語を話さなければなりません。
Kurasu de wa nihongo o hanasanakereba narimasen.

b. クラスでは日本語を話さなければいけません。
Kurasu de wa nihongo o hanasanakereba ikemasen.

There is a subtle difference between (1a) and (1b), however. *Nakereba naranai* (e.g., (1a)) tends to be used when the speaker states his/her own sense of obligation. *Nakareba ikenai* (e.g., (1b)), on the other hand, tends to be used when the sense of obligation is directed toward the hearer—i.e., when the speaker wants to impose a certain obligation on the hearer. (1a) then has the sense of 'I must/ We must/One must speak Japanese in class,' while (1b) has the sense of 'You must speak Japanese in class.'

Note that one can use *nakereba ikenai* about one's own actions. In such a case, a sense of obligation is stronger than in the case of *nakereba naranai*, with the sense of "I absolutely must do ...."

46. *O -SURU* vs. *-TE SASHIAGERU*

[*O* Vstem *ni naru*] and [*o* Vstem *suru*] are so-called respect and humble forms.

(1) a. 先生はもうお帰りになりました。
Sensei wa moo okaeri ni narimashita.
'The teacher has already gone home.'

b. お荷物お持ちしましょう。
O-nimotsu omochi shimashoo.
'I will carry your luggage.'

(1a) directly refers to the action of the teacher, to whom respect is due, while it is the speaker's action that is referred to in (1b).

There is an important restriction on the usage of [*o -suru*]. This form is used only when the action of the speaker (or the speaker's in-group) has some beneficial effect on the person, to whom respect is due and action is directed. In (1b), the speaker's carrying luggage would be a definite benefit for the addressee. Sentences like (2a) and (2b) are unacceptable in normal situations since the speaker's action does not have any beneficial consequence.

(2)　a．＊ビールをお飲みしましょう。
　　　　＊*Biiru o onomi shimashoo.*
　　　　'I will drink beer (for you).'
　　　b．＊私がお帰りしましょう。
　　　　＊*Watashi ga okaeri shimashoo.*
　　　　'I will go home (for you).'

(2a) is acceptable only if the addressee is trying to get rid of beer or the like.

Now, when the speaker offers to do a similar favor for someone who is an intimate friend, a family member, or one's inferior, one would use *-te ageru*.

(3)　その荷物，持ってあげようか。
　　　Sono nimotsu, motte ageyoo ka.
　　　'Shall I carry your luggage ?'
(4)　今日はてんぷらを作ってあげましょう。
　　　Kyoo wa tenpura o tsukutte agemashoo.
　　　'I will cook tempura (for you) today.'

The polite version *-te sashiageru* can be used when the person one is doing a favor for requires respect, as in (5).

(5)　先生にてんぷらを作ってさしあげました。
　　　Sensei ni tenpura o tsukutte sashiagemashita.
　　　'I cooked tempura for the teacher.'

Now, compare the following sentences.

(6)   a．あとで，お送りしましょう。
       Ato de ookuri shimashoo.
     b．あとで送ってさしあげましょう。
       Ato de okutte sashiagemashoo.
       'I will send (it) later (for you).'

In making an offer to do something to someone superior or to whom formality is due, one should use *o -suru* as in (6a). *-Te sashiageru* in such cases too directly implies a favor being done, and thus is impolite. Of course, if one is reporting what one did for the teacher, for example, the use of *-te sashiageru* is fine.

47. *YOO TO SURU* vs. *YOO NI SURU*

Verb (tentative form) + *to suru* and Verb (dictionary form) + *yoo ni suru* are often both translated to English 'try to do such and such'. These two expressions, however, mean quite different things. Observe the following sentences.

(1)   a．御飯を食べようとしましたが，どうしても食べられませんでした。
       Gohan o tabeyoo to shimashita ga, dooshitemo taberaremasen deshita.
       'I tried to eat but I could not eat.'
     b．御飯を食べようとしたところへ電話がかかってきて，食べられませんでした。
       Gohan o tabeyoo to shita tokoro e denwa ga kakatte kite, taberaremasen deshita.
       'When I was about to eat, there was a telephone call, so I

could not eat.'

(2) 御飯を食べる暇もないほど忙しかったが，なるべく御飯を
食べるようにしました。

*Gohan o taberu hima mo nai hodo isogashikatta ga,
narubeku gohan o taberu yoo ni shimashita.*

'I was so busy that I hardly had any time to eat, but I tried to
eat.'

As (1) indicates, *tabeyoo to suru* has the connotation that the
speaker tried to eat but was not successful. *Taberu yoo ni suru*, on
the other hand, implies that the speaker made an honest effort to eat,
and hence was successful at an attempt.

Since verb (tentative) + *to suru* implies an unsuccessful attempt to
do something, this pattern would be inappropriate as a request.

(3) a . *パーティーへ行こうとして下さい。
  *Paatii e ikoo to shite kudasai.
  b . パーティーへ行くようにして下さい。
  Paatii e iku yoo ni shite kudasai.
  'Please try to go to the party.'

NEGATIVE EXPRESSIONS

48. *NAIDE* vs. *NAKUTE* ───────────────────

While adjectives and copula have only one negative gerund form
——*nakute*, verbal gerund can be negated either by *nakute* or *naide*.

(1) a. 寒く $\left\{\begin{array}{l} なくて, \\ *ないで, \end{array}\right\}$ いい。

Samuku- $\left\{\begin{array}{l} nakute, \\ *naide, \end{array}\right\}$ ii.

'It's not cold, and so it's good.'

b. きれいじゃ $\left\{\begin{array}{l} なくて, \\ *ないで, \end{array}\right\}$ 値段も高い。

Kirei-ja- $\left\{\begin{array}{l} nakute, \\ *naide, \end{array}\right\}$ nedan mo takai.

'It's not pretty and the price is also high.'

c. 病気じゃ $\left\{\begin{array}{l} なくて, \\ *ないで, \end{array}\right\}$ ちょっと疲れているだけだ。

Byooki-ja $\left\{\begin{array}{l} nakute, \\ *naide, \end{array}\right\}$ chotto tsukarete iru dake da.

'I am not sick. I am only a little tired.'

d. 学生が予習を $\left\{\begin{array}{l} しなくて, \\ しないで, \end{array}\right\}$ 困ります。

Gakusei ga yoshuu o $\left\{\begin{array}{l} shi-nakute, \\ shi-naide, \end{array}\right\}$ komarimasu.

'My students do not do homework, and I am troubled,'

In some cases, however, the *nakute* form is inappropriate for verbs, as in (2) - (6).

(2) 勉強 $\left\{ \begin{array}{l} しないで \\ *しなくて \end{array} \right\}$ クラスへ来た。

Benkyoo $\left\{ \begin{array}{l} shi\text{-}naide \\ *shi\text{-}nakute \end{array} \right\}$ kurasu e kita.

'(He) came to class without having prepared.'

(3) くつをぬが $\left\{ \begin{array}{l} ないで \\ *なくて \end{array} \right\}$ 家へ入った。

Kutsu o nug- $\left\{ \begin{array}{l} anaide \\ *anakute \end{array} \right\}$ uchi e haitta.

'(He) entered the house without taking his shoes off.'

(4) 図書館へ行か $\left\{ \begin{array}{l} ないで \\ *なくて \end{array} \right\}$ 家で勉強した。

Toshokan e ik- $\left\{ \begin{array}{l} anaide \\ *anakute \end{array} \right\}$ uchi de benkyoo shita.

'(I) studied at home instead of going to the library.'

(5) 日本へ行か $\left\{ \begin{array}{l} ないで \\ *なくて \end{array} \right\}$ ほしい。

Nihon e ik- $\left\{ \begin{array}{l} anaide \\ *anakute \end{array} \right\}$ hoshii.

'I don't want (you) to go to Japan.'

(6) 日本へ行か $\left\{ \begin{array}{l} ないで \\ *なくて \end{array} \right\}$ 下さい。

Nihon e ik- $\left\{ \begin{array}{l} anaide \\ *anakute \end{array} \right\}$ kudasai.

'Please don't go to Japan.'

What is common to sentences (2) - (6) is that S_1 and S_2 in [S_1 *naide* S_2] form a tightly knit unit in that S_1 is felt to be subordinated to S_2. In (5) and (6), S_1 and S_2 are so tightly knit that they form single verb phrases. In (2) and (3), S_1 serves as an adverbial clause to S_2. (2)

indicates that the manner in which (he) came to class is "without having done the homework." In (3), the manner in which (he) entered a house is "without taking his shoes off." In (4), there is a strong semantic tie between S₁ and S₂ in that the choice is between going to the library and studying at home.

With *nakute*, on the other hand, S₁ and S₂ are not *a priori* related. S₁ and S₂ stand independent of each other.

    (7) 田中さんが来なくて，困った。

         Tanaka-san ga ko-nakute, komatta.

         'Mr. Tanaka did not come, and I was troubled.'

    (8) 先生の質問に答えられなくて，先生にしかられた。

         Sensei no shitsumon ni kotae-rare-nakute, sensei ni shi-karareta.

         'I could not answer the teacher's questions, and I was scolded by the teacher.'

Sentence (7) simply states that Tanaka did not come, and as a consequence, (I) was in trouble. Sentence (8) states that (I) could not answer the question and so (I) was scolded. In other words, [S₁-neg] and [S₂] are merely juxtaposed. Juxtaposing two sentences often results in a "causal" interpretation between the two sentences. Hence, *nakute* often gives a sense that S₁ is the reason/cause for S₂.

BIBLIOGRAPHY

Kitagawa (1984), Kuno (1975), McGloin (1986)

49. *NAIDE IRU* vs. *TE INAI*

The Verb-*te iru* form can be negated either by *naide iru* or *te inai* as in (1) and (2).

(1) 食べないでいる。
Tabenaide iru.
'I haven't eaten.'

(2) 食べていない。
Tabete inai.
'I haven't eaten.'

Sentence (1) implies that the person has intentionally abstained from eating——perhaps because he is on a hunger strike. Sentence (2), on the other hand, simply denies that one has eaten.

Such intention or volition is a general feature of *naide* followed by verbs such as *hoshii, oku, morau,* etc.

(3) a . 戸をしめないでおいた。
To o shimenaide oita.
'I left the door unclosed.'

b . 戸をしめておかなかった。
To o shimete okanakatta.
'I didn't close the door.'

(4) a . 見ないでもらった。
Minaide moratta.
'I had (him) not look.'

b . 見てもらわなかった。
Mite morawanakatta.
'I didn't have (him) look.'

Sentence (3a) can be used, for example, when the speaker intentionally kept the door open so that someone could get in. Sentence (3b) might be used when the speaker did not close the door, and hence some robber got into the house.

50. *NAI HAZU DA* vs. *HAZU WA NAI*

Hazu da 'supposed to, expected to' can be negated either by placing a negative morpheme before or after *hazu*, as in (1) and (2).

(1) 田中さんは来ないはずだ。
Tanaka-san wa konai hazu da.
'Mr. Tanaka is not expected to come——I am almost sure he won't come.'

(2) 田中さんは来るはずがない。
Tanaka-san wa kuru hazu ga nai.
'There is no likelihood that Mr. Tanaka will come.'

Sentence (1) implies that the speaker conjectures with some certainty that Tanaka will not be coming. With (1), however, there is always a possibility that it will turn out otherwise. So, one can say (3).

(3) 田中さんは来ないはずだったが、来た。
Tanaka-san wa konai hazu datta ga, kita.
'Mr. Tanaka was not supposed to come, but he came.'

Sentence (2), on the other hand, negates even the possibility that Tanaka might come and gives a strong negative assertion. Hence, in the following context, *hazu ga nai* is preferred.

(4) 一度もやったことがなかったから、やれるはずがなかった。
Ichido mo yatta koto ga nakatta kara, yareru hazu ga nakatta.
'Since I had never done that before, I could not possibly be expected to be able to do it.'

(5) 練習しなければ、上手になるはずがない。
Renshuu shinakereba, joozu ni naru hazu ga nai.
'If you don't practice, you cannot possibly be expected to improve.'

BIBLIOGRAPHY

Akatsuka, Noriko. 1985. "Conditionals and the Epistemic Scale." *Language* 61. 3: 625-639.

Alfonso, Anthony. 1966. *Japanese Language Patterns.* Tokyo: Sophia University.

Backhouse, A. E. & H. C. Quackenbush. 1979. "Aspects of *uchi* constructions." *Papers in Japanese Linguistics* 6: 51-86.

Harada, S. I. 1976. "Honorifics." in *Syntax and Semantics 5: Japanese Generative Grammar*, ed. by M. Shibatani, 499-561. New York: Academic Press.

Hinds, John. 1973. "Anaphoric Demonstratives in Japanese." *Journal of the Association of Teachers of Japanese* 8. 2-3: 1-14.

Inoue, Kazuko (ed.) 1983. *Nihongo no Kihon Koozoo.* Tokyo: Sanseido.

Jorden, Eleanor H. 1963. *Beginning Japanese.* New Haven: Yale University Press.

Josephs, Lewis. 1976. "Complementation," in *Syntax and Semantics 5: Japanese Generative Grammar*, ed. by M. Shibatani, 307-370. New York: Academic Press.

Kashioka, Tamako. 1980. "Yoo-da to Rashii ni kansuru Ichi Koosatsu." *Nihongo Kyoiku* 41: 169-178.

Kitagawa, Chisato. 1984. "On the Two Forms of Negative Gerund in Japanese." in *Studies in Japasese Language Use*, ed. by C. Kitagawa & S. Miyagawa, 89-126. Edmonton: Linguistic Research.

Kunihiro, Tetsuya. 1982. *Imiron no Hoohoo.* Tokyo: Taishukan.

————. 1984. " 'No da' no Igiso Oboegaki." *Tokyo Daigaku Gengogaku Ronshu*, pp. 5-9.

Kunihiro, Tetsuya, *et al.* 1982. *Kotoba no Imi*, 3. Tokyo: Heibonsha.

Kuno, Susumu. 1973. *The Structure of the Japanese Language.* Cambridge, MA: MIT Press.

————. 1975. "Notes on Japanese Sentence Patterns." in *Harvard Studies in Syntax and Semantics I*, ed. by S. Kuno, 405-66. Cambridge, MA: Harvard University.

————. 1976. "The Speaker's Empathy and Its Effect on Syntax: A Reexamination of Yaru and Kureru in Japasese." *Journal of the Association of Teachers of Japanese* 11. 2-3: 249-271.

Kuno, Susumu & Tazuko Monane. 1979. "Positioning of Quantifier-like Particles." *Journal of the Association of Teachers of Japanese* 14. 2: 115-140.

Makino, Seiichi. 1975-76. "On the Nature of the Japanese Potential Construction." *Papers in Japanese Linguistics* 4: 97-124.

Makino, Seiichi & Michio Tsutsui. 1986. *A Dictionary of Basic Japanese Grammar.* Tokyo: The Japan Times.

McGloin, Naomi Hanaoka. 1976-77. "The Speaker's Attitude and the Conditionals *to, tara* and *ba.*" *Papers in Japanese Linguistics* 5: 181-191.

————. 1980. "Some Observations Concerning No Desu Expressions." *Journal of the Association of Teachers of Japanese* 15. 2: 117-149.

————. 1985. "*No*-pronominalization in Japanese." *Papers in Japanese Linguistics* 10: 1-15.

————. 1986. *Negation in Japanese.* Edmonton: Boreal Scholarly Publishers.

Miura, Akira. 1974. "The V-ru Form vs. the V-ta Form." *Papers in Japanese Linguistics* 3: 95-122.

Miyagawa, Shigeru. 1984. "Pragmatics of Causation in Japanese." in *Studies in Japanese Language Use,* ed. by C. Kitagawa & S. Miyagawa, 147-184. Edmonton: Linguistic Research.

Morita, Yoshiyuki. 1971. "The Usage of -dake and -bakari." *Bulletin of the Institute of Language Teaching* (Waseda Univ.) 10: 1-27.

————. 1977, 1980, 1984. *Kiso Nihongo,* Vol. 1-3. Tokyo: Kadokawa Shoten.

————. 1983. *Nihongo no Hyoogen.* Tokyo: Sorinsha.

————. 1984. *Nihongo no Hassoo.* Tokyo: Tojusha.

————. 1985. *Goyoo Bun no Bunseki to Kenkyuu.* Tokyo: Meiji Shoin.

Nakau, Minoru. 1976. "Tense, Aspect, and Modality." in *Syntax and Semantics 5: Japanese Generative Grammar,* ed. by M. Shibatani, 421-482. New York: Academic Press.

Shibatani, Masayoshi. 1967. "Causativization." in *Syntax and Semantics 5: Japanese Generative Grammar,* ed. by M. Shibatani, 239-294. New York: Academic Press.

Simon, Mutsuko Endo. 1986-87. *Supplementary Grammar Notes to an Introduction to Modern Japanese.* Ann Arbor: Center for Japanese Studies, University of Michigan.

Soga, Matsuo. 1976. "The Structure of Negation and Delimitational Particles in Japanese." *Journal of the Association of Teachers of Japanese* 11. 1: 65-84.

————. 1983. *Tense and Aspect in Modern Colloquial Japanese.* Vancouver: Univ. of British Columbia Press.

Suzuki, Shinobu. 1978. *Kyoshiyo Nihongo Kyoiku Handobukku 3, Bunpo 1, Joshi no Shomondai.* Tokyo: The Japan Foundation.

Terakura, Hiroko. 1983. "Noun Modification and the Use of *To Yuu.*" *Journal of the Association of Teachers of Japanese* 18. 1: 23-55.

————. 1985. "English *before*-clauses and Japanese Temporal Clauses." *Journal of Asian Culture* 9: 199-215.

Uyeno, Tazuko. 1971. "A Study of Japanese Modality——A performative Analysis of Sentence Particles." University of Michigan Ph. D. Dissertation.

INDEX

A STUDENTS' GUIDE TO JAPANESE GRAMMAR
［英文］ 間違えやすい日本語語法

©Naomi Hanaoka McGloin 1989
NDC815/xx, 147p/21cm

初版第 1 刷——1989年 2 月15日
第10刷——2013年 9 月 1 日

著　者　マクグロイン花岡直美

発行者　鈴木　一行

発行所　　株式会社　大修館書店

〒113-8541　東京都文京区湯島 2-1-1
電話　03-3868-2651（販売部）　03-3868-2294（編集部）
［出版情報］http://www.taishukan.co.jp

製版・印刷・製本／図書印刷　　　　装幀／吉野富士彦
ISBN978-4-469-22065-0　　　　Printed in Japan